LORD OF THE MARKETPLACE

LORD OF THE MARKETPLACE

MYRON RUSH

VICTOR BOOKS®

A DIVISION OF SCRIPTURE PRESS PUBLICATIONS INC.
USA CANADA ENGLAND

Second printing, 1988

Most Scripture taken from the *Holy Bible, New International Version,*
© 1973, 1978, 1984, International Bible Society. Used by permission of
Zondervan Bible Publishers. Other quotations are from *The Living Bible*
(TLB), © 1971 Tyndale House Publishers, Wheaton, IL 60189, and from the
Revised Standard Version of the Bible (RSV), © 1946, 1952, 1971, 1973.
Used by permission.

Recommended Dewey Decimal Classification: 248.88

Suggested Subject Heading: PERSONAL CHRISTIANITY FOR WORKING AND
PROFESSIONAL CLASSES

Library of Congress Catalog Card Number: 85-63317
ISBN: 0-89693-278-8

VICTOR BOOKS
A division of SP Publications, Inc.
P.O. Box 1825 · Wheaton, Illinois 60189

Contents

This book is dedicated to the Fellowship of Companies for Christ and to the great work they're doing in helping Christian business owners and chief executive officers around the country discover and personally apply biblical principles of business on a daily basis.

Introduction

What does it mean to be a Christian business person? For years I thought it meant: I run my business *better than* non-Christians. That philosophy led me to adopt a "better-than" attitude and approach to business. I worked hard to make sure I did things "better than" the non-Christian community. I had better trained sales people, higher quality products, and the best credit references. I tried to make my business a showcase that was better than any in the non-Christian community—after all, that was my "witness" for God.

This philosophy seems to be rather common among conscientious Christian business people. I've found that many desire to use their businesses as a witness for the Lord. But there's a problem with this viewpoint.

During a management seminar a businessman told me, "I keep the landscaping around my place of business looking better than any business in my area. That helps communicate to people what a Christian stands for."

Maybe it does. But it also might communicate that the owner simply has a green thumb and enjoys gardening. The simple fact is, when we adopt a "better-than" approach to being a Christian witness in the marketplace, we run the risk of becoming heirs to the Pharisees.

The Pharisees were the religious leaders of their day. They had large sections of the Old Testament memorized and people looked to them as examples of godliness.

But their entire religious philosophy was based on the idea that they did things *better than* other people. They prayed better than others. They fasted better than others. They gave gifts better than others. They knew God better than others. They knew how to live better than others.

Yet Matthew notes that Jesus spent quite a bit of time condemning the Pharisees for their "better-than" attitudes and actions. At one point He charged that "Everything they do is done for men to see" (Matt. 23:5).

Thus when we attempt to witness for Christ by conducting our businesses "better than" the non-Christian community, we risk falling into the same trap the Pharisees did. Not only were they committed to doing things better, they wanted to make sure others *knew* what they did was better. As a result, their religious pride got in the way and they wound up promoting themselves rather than God. The "better-than" approach to being a Christian witness in the marketplace can cause us to do the same thing. I speak from experience. I used to operate that way.

There is one other problem with the "better-than" approach that deserves mention. While I practiced this approach in the marketplace in an effort to provide a Christian witness, I must admit that I also wanted to use biblical principles of business and ethics because I thought it would be "good for business." You see, once I discovered that biblical business principles worked, I wanted to implement them so my business would be more profitable. My real objective, then, was to use godly principles to make more earthly money.

The Apostle Paul criticized people "who think that godliness is a means to financial gain" (1 Tim. 6:5). He also pointed out that the lover of money is "conceited and understands nothing" (1 Tim. 6:4).

From this passage, we can see that God obviously is not happy with us when we selfishly use biblical principles just to promote our own interests. God wants our obedience because we love Him, not because we're trying to use Him. When we use the Bible for selfish gain we are no better than the Pharisees, of whom Jesus said, "These people honor Me with their lips, but their hearts are far from Me" (Mark 7:6).

Being a Christian business person doesn't involve doing things "better than" the non-Christian community. It doesn't even necessarily entail the use of biblical principles of business. Many people use biblical principles of business without even recognizing their true source.

So what *is* distinctive about the Christian in business? Basically, being a Christian business person means *we do business differently* from the way the non-Christian does. The purpose of this book is to describe that difference.

MYRON D. RUSH
PRESIDENT
MANAGEMENT TRAINING SYSTEMS

1
The Battle for
the Business World

Don Skinner, the owner of a small electronics manufacturing company, sat across the dinner table from me. He was wearing an expensive, beautifully tailored, three-piece suit. In fact, *everything* he wore looked expensive—from his highly polished shoes and French-cuffed silk shirt to the diamond-studded writing pen he was using to "run the numbers" on his latest business deal. In short, he looked like Madison Avenue's ideal of the successful businessman.

"Myron," he said with a sheepish smile, "I know some of the people at church might think I'm being unethical, but the stakes were just too high to lose this one."

Don explained that he had "been forced" to bribe a company's purchasing agent in order to land a large contract he'd been working on for several months.

"I didn't have much choice," he continued. "My competition was trying to buy them off to get the contract. The client even came to me and said he wanted to do business with my company, but I would have to beat my competition's offer. It was just too good a deal to pass up. So I *beat* their offer."

The longer Don talked, the more defensive he became. "Look," he said, frustration and anger showing in his voice, "I'm a businessman—not a theologian. You know yourself that it's a dog-eat-dog world out there. Anyway, I look at it this way. As a businessman, I feel my job is to make the money needed to support the church. The more money I make, the more I can give to God's work. And I sure don't see anybody turning it down when the offering plate is passed." He gave a half sarcastic chuckle.

A few minutes later, however, his tone changed. "Sometimes I feel trapped between what the Bible teaches and the way I'm required to act in order to successfully run my business," he said.

As we finished our cheesecake and the last cup of coffee, Don looked me straight in the eye. Then he posed the question that motivated me to write this book. "Myron," he asked, *"how can you be a good Christian and a good businessman at the same time?"*

As I drove home from my meeting with Don, I realized that a multitude of Christians must also feel trapped as they attempt to incorporate biblical principles into their business lives. Many times I'd heard business people ask similar questions at the management seminars I conduct around the country.

As Don said, it *is* a "dog-eat-dog world" out there. The pressures on business people today are greater than ever before. While we search for excellence on the one hand, the competitive nature of free enterprise and the capitalistic system frequently tempts us to look for shortcuts and compromises on the other.

As a result, both Christians and non-Christians often find themselves doing things in the name of "good business" that they would never consider doing outside the context of their jobs. Yet at times, the desire to fulfill business' burning goal—to get the best possible return on one's investment—compels us to compromise.

For example, Betty Collins, the owner of a beauty salon once told me, 'There are lots of ways to get even with Uncle Sam in my business, and I used to use all of them. As a Christian I am strongly against cheating, but I used to justify cheating on my income taxes."

She shook her head and went on to say, "I tried to ease my conscience by telling myself the government wasted too much money on giveaway programs I didn't approve of. Therefore, it was OK to cheat on my taxes. I even tried to convince myself it wasn't really cheating. I was just keeping what was mine anyway."

The Purpose of This Book

Simply stated, the purpose of this book is to answer Don's question, "How can you be a *good* Christian and a *good* business person at the same time?" Practically speaking, the answer is not all that simple. In fact, for some of you, this book may raise more questions than it answers. And some of you (a limited number, I hope!) may find yourselves disagreeing with some of the main points I'll present here.

Still, I hope this book will motivate you and me to do four things:

(1) Take a new look at the way we currently are conducting

our business affairs—and why;

(2) Closely examine the biblical principles that apply to doing business in today's marketplace;

(3) Spend time evaluating how the biblical principles of business presented in this book relate to our specific, current situations; and

(4) Apply the biblical principles presented in this book as God directs us individually.

My prayer is that God will use this book in your life, as He is using it in mine, so that we truly can make Him the Lord of *our* marketplace.

Is God Really Interested in Business?

While I was growing up on a farm in rural Oklahoma, my father told me, "Son, you'll never get ahead in this world working for the other fella." Then he would ruffle my hair (I had hair then) with his big, burly hand and say, "Instead of working *for* the owner, you've got to *be* the owner. That's the only way you'll ever have anything."

At an early age I decided I wanted to follow my father's advice instead of his example. He had worked hard for the "owner" all his life, and sure enough, we never seemed to have much.

At the ripe old age of eight, therefore, I decided it was time to start my own business. One morning I walked into the kitchen where my mother was baking bread and announced, "I'm going to be a businessman." My mother smiled as she patted flour from her hands into my hair and said, "That's nice."

I realized that every entrepreneur had to have a product, so I looked around our poor dirt farm for a product I could use to start my business. I also figured that a good business person had to know a great deal about his business. So after about a week of thinking over my options (which weren't many), I decided to sell fishing worms.

I chose fishing worms for two reasons. First, the manure pile behind our barn grew some of the biggest and best worms I had ever seen. And second, I seemed to be able to catch more fish from the pond on our farm than any of the other boys in our small community could. Accordingly, I concluded that I probably had the best fishing worms around, and that I knew more about catching fish with them than anyone else in the neighborhood.

The next Saturday morning I found an old board and some paint, made a sign that said, "Worms for sale—10¢," and nailed it to a fence post near the road in front of our house.

I remember sitting under a shade tree in the front yard all day, waiting for people to come flocking up the long driveway to buy my wonderful worms. I had visions of pulling my little red wagon—heaped high with money—into the bank, and being rich! In my mind I had already spent the money on things my parents could not afford to buy me; things like a new bicycle, a BB gun, a new baseball glove, and a real bat. The list went on and on.

My first attempt at business ended in total failure, however. I didn't sell a single worm. Why? Because I had overlooked the simple fact that everyone in my community had his own manure pile behind his barn—and each pile had an adequate supply of worms. People who *didn't* have manure piles never came out this way to buy worms anyway.

By late afternoon I was crushed. All my hopes of instant wealth and buying new toys were suddenly gone. Even at that young age I felt the pain and frustration of failing at business. Finally I got up, and after angrily kicking the shade tree, I walked into the house—crying.

As my mother held me in her arms, I told her no one had stopped to buy my worms, and that now I wasn't going to be able to buy all the things I had planned. I will never forget her response.

"Myron," she said, as she held me on her knee, "did you pray and ask Jesus to help you with your new business?"

"No!" I exclaimed, as I climbed off her lap and ran back outside. I hadn't done that—and I thought I had a very logical reason for my decision. In fact, I still remember the thoughts that went through my mind at that moment: *Surely, Jesus is too busy with other more important church stuff than to be interested in my worm business.* Then I rationalized, *God is only interested in religious stuff. Since business isn't religious stuff, God certainly couldn't be interested in business.*

The point of this whole story is this: Over the years, I have discovered that similar thoughts have gone through the minds of most adults sometime during their business careers. As I encourage people to let God get more personally involved in their business affairs, I frequently am told, "God has more important things to do than think about my business problems."

Every time I hear someone make that comment I think back to my first business venture—selling fishing worms as an eight-year-old—and I am convinced that Satan is the originator of this lie. He wants to control the business world and all those in it. He certainly doesn't want people asking God's opinion and getting His help with their businesses.

God Is a Businessman

From the first book of the Bible to the last, we see continuous references being made to business life. God showed His concern for the agricultural business when He promised, "As long as the earth endures, seedtime and harvest...will never cease" (Gen. 8:22). In fact, a great deal of Moses' writings in the Old Testament consisted of God's instructions about the farming business. Today farmers understand the importance of periodically letting farm land lie idle or "fallow" for a season to allow the soil to rebuild itself. But in Leviticus, God *already* was saying, "For six years sow your fields, and for six years prune your vineyards and gather their crops. But in the seventh year the land is to have a sabbath of rest" (Lev. 25:3-4).

God also was involved in the real estate business. Several Old Testament passages outline God's instructions on how to conduct real estate transactions (Lev. 25:10-25; Deut. 19:14; 27:17).

In addition, God was interested in the development of a credit and banking system (Ex. 22:25); weights and measures (Lev. 19:35-36); the development of the judicial system (Ex. 23:1-9); and welfare programs to aid the poor (Lev. 19:9-10; Deut. 24:17-22).

God wants business owners to pay their employees proper wages (Deut. 24:15; Jer. 22:13; James 5:4). In fact, as we will see, God is interested in *every* area of business life.

But so is Satan.

The Christian Business Person's Dilemma

At the beginning of this chapter we met Don Skinner— business owner, Christian, and very frustrated and confused person. He was caught between God's principles of business and the world's. He found it impossible to please both. That's why he said, "Sometimes I feel trapped between what the Bible teaches and the way I'm required to act in order to successfully run my business."

Eventually every Christian working in the business world experiences Don's frustration. Once a person becomes a Christian his goals change. He now wants to serve and please Christ instead of self. As *The Living Bible* puts it, "When someone becomes a Christian he becomes a brand-new person inside. He is not the same any more. A new life has begun!" (2 Cor. 5:17, TLB)

Paul expands on this idea by saying, "Don't copy the behavior and customs of this world, but be a new and different person with a fresh newness in all you do and think" (Rom. 12:2, TLB). He also tells us,

> "You were taught, with regard to your former way of life, to put off your old self, which is being corrupted by its deceitful desires; to be made new in the attitude of your minds; and to put on the new self, created to be like God in true righteousness and holiness" (Eph. 4:22-24).

Yes, that is the goal of every Christian. We are to be different from the world and the way it operates. We are to be different persons. Once we become Christians our goal is to please God, not self. As you can see from these verses, the Christian is to differ from the non-Christian. And if that's true, then you would expect the Christian to do business differently from the rest of the business community.

The business world's goal is to succeed in business. As we will discuss in detail in a later chapter, everyone knows that making more money than you spend is the key to success in any business. Therefore, the world's popular philosophy is, *Do whatever it takes to make money, because money is the key to business success.*

That is the source of great frustration for many Christians in business. On one hand, our goal is to serve, obey, and please God—and God says we are to be honest and fair in our business dealings. In fact, we're to treat people as we would want to be treated. On the other hand, as Don observed, "It's a dog-eat-dog world out there," and for the most part, the rest of the business community is committed to doing whatever it takes to succeed in business. Their motto often is, *Do it unto others before they do it unto you!*

As a result, the Christian business person finds himself pulled in two directions. He or she wants to serve, obey, and please God. But he is also sometimes tempted to forget God, roll up his sleeves, and do whatever it takes to compete successfully for business. At the beginning of this chapter we saw Don Skinner doing just that.

Unfortunately, most of us who are Christian business people find ourselves from time to time falling short of what God expects from us as His representatives in the marketplace. Paul, himself a businessman (a tentmaker by trade), explained the problem this way to the Christians in Rome:

> It seems to be a fact of life that when I want to do what is right, I inevitably do what is wrong. I love to do God's will so far as my new nature is concerned; but there is something else deep within me, in my lower nature, that is at war with my mind and wins the fight and makes me a slave to the sin that is still within me. In my mind I want to be God's willing

servant but instead I find myself still enslaved to sin.
So you see how it is: my new life tells me to do
right, but the old nature that is still inside me loves
to sin. Oh, what a terrible predicament I'm in! Who
will free me from my slavery to this deadly lower
nature? (Rom. 7:21-24, TLB)

Most of the Christian business people I know can readily
identify with Paul's frustration in this passage. Like Paul, they
"want to be God's willing servant." But often they also feel
imprisoned by their "lower nature." And like Don Skinner,
they feel "trapped" between wanting to obey God and wanting
to compete effectively in a marketplace where God's laws and
principles of business are not considered. They assume they
can't do both.

Jack McDonnald, the owner of a construction company
which specializes in building small commercial buildings, put
it this way: "It's hard enough being a Christian and standing
up for what is right out there in the world. But it's even harder
trying to incorporate Christian principles into your business,
to be an honest businessman, and to follow your conscience
when it appears most of your competition doesn't even *have*
a conscience."

He told me how a large construction company wanted to
subcontract with his company to build a commercial warehouse facility for a major department store chain. "I really
need the work," he said. "But they're trying to make me
violate the local building codes on the foundation, electrical,
and heating systems in order to keep the costs down. They
discovered the bid was too low and they're trying to cut
corners any way they can to save money."

As I write this chapter, Jack is still struggling with his

conscience and his checkbook, trying to decide what to do.

Jack certainly could understand what Paul was talking about when he said, "I love to do God's will so far as my new nature is concerned; but there is something else deep within me, in my lower nature, that is at war with my mind" (Rom. 7:22-23, TLB).

During a management seminar, Steve Crane—the owner of a bank in the southeast—said, "Before I became a Christian it was a lot easier to make banking decisions. All I needed to know was, Will the deal make us money? Now I have to evaluate whether or not the deal fits within biblical guidelines, and whether or not it's even God's will for me to get involved. Sometimes some of my vice-presidents think I've lost my mind when I turn down a good money-making opportunity because it violates biblical principles."

He laughed and continued, "And I'm sure they think I'm nuts when sometimes I tell them I'll have to pray about it before I can give them my answer."

As Steve indicated, most non-Christians simply use money as their criterion for making business decisions. The more money there is to be made, the better the business deal. Even though the Christian uses money as one criterion for making business decisions, he also uses God's Word.

Unlike the non-Christian business person, the Christian in business wants to make sure God approves of the transaction. In fact, pleasing God takes precedence over making money.

The War for the Business World

In Romans, Paul writes, "But I see another law at work in the members of my body, waging war against the law of my mind and making me a prisoner of the law of sin at work within my members" (7:23).

Paul is talking about a war going on within us—a war between the forces of God that encourage us to do what is right, and the forces of Satan that tempt us to do what is wrong.

In Ephesians, Paul expands on the nature of this war:

> For we are not fighting against people made of flesh and blood, but against persons without bodies—the evil rulers of the unseen world, those mighty satanic beings and great evil princes of darkness who rule this world; and against huge numbers of wicked spirits in the spirit world (6:12, TLB).

In this passage we discover the Christian is not only in a war, but he is fighting against Satan himself and his host of demons. This passage also tells us that Satan is the ruler of this natural world. In fact, Scripture calls him "the god of this evil world" (2 Cor. 4:4, TLB).

In Luke's Gospel we see Satan offering Christ control of the world's marketplaces if only He'll worship Satan and recognize him as the supreme god of the universe:

> Then Satan took Him up and revealed to Him all the kingdoms of the world in a moment of time; and the devil told Him, "I will give You all these splendid kingdoms and their glory—for they are mine to give to anyone I wish—if You will only get down on Your knees and worship me." Jesus replied, "We must worship God, and Him alone. So it is written in the Scriptures" (Luke 4:5-8, TLB).

Notice that this passage points out that Satan is in control of the kingdoms (marketplaces) of the world and that he can put anyone he pleases in charge of them. And how does Satan control these marketplaces? By controlling the *people* who operate them. And how does he control the people in charge of the marketplaces of the world? By deceiving them.

From the beginning of history, Satan has deceived humankind. Eve admitted, "The serpent [Satan] deceived me" (Gen. 3:13). And the Apostle John indicates that Satan will continue to "deceive the nations in the four corners of the earth" until God destroys him (Rev. 20:7-8).

Not only does Satan realize the way to control the world is to control its marketplaces; he has a plan to accomplish this. God's Word exposes the nature of this plan:

He also forced everyone, small and great, rich and poor, free and slave, to receive a mark on his right hand or on his forehead, so that no one could buy or sell unless he had the mark (Rev. 13:16-17).

Notice what Satan will do. First, he will *"force everyone,* small and great, rich and poor, free and slave." In other words, there won't be any options or alternatives to falling in line with Satan's plan. Everyone will be forced into his program for the business community.

Second, people will have to register with him by receiving some type of identifying mark. Notice the purpose of the mark: "So that *no one* could *buy* or *sell* unless he had the mark."

Do you understand the significance of that verse? Someday Satan will make it impossible to do business of any kind— buying or selling— unless people are registered with him and recognize him as the all-powerful god of this world!

Think of it. No matter how rich or poor people are, no

matter how big or small their businesses (they may own multimillion dollar corporations or mom and pop shops), they won't be able to *buy* or *sell* unless they receive Satan's mark and openly recognize him as ruler of this world.

Satan is extremely clever. He knows the way to control people is to control their pocketbooks. If you can control all buying and selling, you can control all people.

The Christian business person, however, can play a key role in stifling Satan's plans to become Lord of the Marketplace. Scripture plainly states that "the good influence of godly citizens causes a city to prosper, but the moral decay of the wicked drives it downhill" (Prov. 11:11, TLB).

This verse points out how valuable godly people are to a society. When the Lord's people follow His principles, the entire society benefits and profits. When people ignore God's principles, society suffers.

It follows that Christian business people everywhere must take a strong stand for God in the marketplace. They must be committed to knowing and applying biblical principles of doing business.

As they do, I believe three things will occur: First, they will prosper. Second, the entire business community—and society in general—will be more prosperous. Third, Satan's effort to control the world by controlling the marketplace will be held back.

What about you? Are you ready to take your stand in the marketplace for God by applying biblical principles in your business or work? The remaining chapters of this book are designed to help you become better equipped to withstand Satan's attacks on you and your business. They're also intended to prepare you to be the kind of business person

God wants you to be.

Jesus tells us, "You are the world's light—a city on a hill, glowing in the night for all to see. Don't hide your light! Let it shine for all; let your good deeds glow for all to see, so that they will praise your Heavenly Father" (Matt. 5:14-16, TLB).

What better place is there to apply this passage than in the marketplaces of the world?

Chapter Summary

The business world is highly competitive. As Don Skinner remarked, it's a "dog-eat-dog world out there." Consequently the extremely competitive atmosphere of the marketplace sometimes tempts the Christian business person to make questionable compromises.

As my friend Don also noted, the Christian business person occasionally feels "trapped" between what the Bible teaches and the pressures to compromise his convictions for the sake of making his business more profitable.

This book is designed to help the Christian business person take a new look at what the Bible teaches about business and to apply those principles as God directs.

Sometimes we may feel God isn't interested in our business and its specific needs. But the Word indicates that God is interested in all types of businesses—from agriculture to law. The Bible also reveals that God is concerned with the way employers treat and pay their employees.

A war is raging in the business world. Paul observes that as Christians, we are engaged in a battle with Satan. We are fighting against "those mighty satanic beings and great evil princes of darkness who rule this world" (Eph. 6:12, TLB). Satan's goal is to control the marketplaces of the world, for in doing so, he can control the world's people.

His plan is described in the Book of Revelation: "He also forced everyone, small and great, rich and poor, free and slave, to receive a mark on his right hand or on his forehead, so that no one could buy or sell unless he had the mark" (Rev. 13:16-17).

Satan's aim, then, is to make it impossible for people to do business of any kind unless they are registered with him and recognize him as the god of this world.

The Christian business person plays a key role in stifling Satan's plans. As Proverbs points out, "The good influence of godly citizens causes a city to prosper, but the moral decay of the wicked drives it downhill" (Prov. 11:11, TLB). And Matthew tells us that Christians are to be a light in the marketplace, pointing the way to God by their good deeds (Matt. 5:14-16).

Personal Application

1. Read Romans 12:2.
    a. Evaluate your business activities over the past few months and identify any actions or behavior which you feel copy the behavior and customs of the world in the marketplace.
    b. What do you think this verse is really saying to the Christian business person?

2. Read Matthew 5:14-16. What are some ways you could more effectively apply this passage in your business?

2
The Role of Money in Business

Question: Why do people go into business for themselves? I can tell you why I've started businesses. I wanted to make money. When I was eight, I saw the worm business as a way to buy all the toys my parents couldn't afford. At the age of thirty-two, I started an asphalt repair business for much the same reason—*to make money*. Only this time, the toys I wanted were a lot bigger and much more expensive. In any business I ever started, the goal was always the same—*to make money*!

If you've ever started your own business, are running your own firm, or are even thinking of launching a business career, I'm sure your goal is the same as mine—*to make money*.

Now, let me ask you another question: How do you determine how well a business is doing? A few years ago a friend and I started a small manufacturing company. The first year we did $250,000 in sales. The next year our sales reached over a million dollars.

We were very excited about our growth. We talked about how much better we had done the second year. Our goal wasn't only to *make* money, but to use money as a measuring stick to determine how *well* our business was doing.

All of these illustrations point to one unavoidable fact: Money is the lifeblood of our society.

The Power of Money

We've all heard the phrase, "Money talks." But have you ever stopped to listen to what it's saying about us? Whether we want to admit it or not, in many instances money is the controlling force over our businesses and our lives.

At a recent management seminar I conducted in Louisiana, one of the topics we covered was "Biblical Principles of Decision-making." As we discussed these principles, a businessman spoke up.

"I don't have trouble making decisions," he said with a laugh. "If it will make me money, I decide yes. If it won't make me money, I decide no. It's as simple as that!"

Most of the decisions a business person makes involve money. We either are deciding how we will make it or how we will spend it. And our goal is always the same: to make more than we spend. Money, therefore, usually becomes the controlling factor in all our business decisions. And if money is controlling our business decisions, isn't it true that it's probably controlling us as well?

As a Christian businessman, I would never want to admit to anyone that money was controlling me. But let me raise one more question: If I allow money to control the kinds of decisions I make, then isn't it true that money is in fact controlling me? I don't know how you answered that question, but my conclusion is yes.

In recent months I have been struggling with this very issue; I hate to admit it, but I am appalled at the influence money has had over me, my business, and my life. I suspect that if you are totally honest with yourself, you might have to confess the same thing.

To break money's spell over us, though, we need to know where it comes from.

The Source of Money and Wealth

Money itself is neither good nor bad. It is in fact a necessity of life in our modern society. It is absolutely essential to conduct business transactions.

The Bible indicates that there are two sources of money and wealth. In Deuteronomy, God tells Israel, "Always remember that it is the Lord your God who gives you power to become rich" (8:18, TLB). It is evident from this verse that the Lord gives people power to make money and acquire wealth.

But the Bible also indicates that *Satan* has the power to give wealth to people. As we saw in the last chapter, Luke's Gospel mentions that Satan offered Jesus the kingdoms of the world; all Christ had to do in return was worship him (Luke 4:5-8). It is important to notice that Jesus didn't contradict Satan's claim to be able to give kingdoms and wealth to anyone he wanted. He did, however, make it very clear to Satan that we are to serve God, "and Him alone" (Luke 4:8, TLB).

In sum, then, it would appear the Bible teaches that the power to get wealth comes either from God or Satan. If we are serving the Lord, our wealth comes from Him. On the other hand, if we are serving Satan, *he* becomes the source of our wealth.

I hope you claim to serve God. Yet it is not enough just to *claim* to serve God. If you are a Christian business person you have the responsibility to serve Him *by your actions.* You need to know what God requires of a person once he or she becomes a Christian. You must learn God's principles for living and begin applying them to every area of your life, including your business.

The Money Trap

Money tends to deceive us by giving us a false sense of security. A multitude of Christian business people (including me—and perhaps even you) have deceived themselves over the years by believing money could meet most if not all of their business needs.

Yet because the business person is so strongly tempted to find his or her security in money, Jesus spent a good deal of time addressing this subject:

> Someone in the crowd said to Him, "Teacher, tell my brother to divide the inheritance with me." Jesus replied, "Man, who appointed Me a judge or an arbiter between you?" Then He said to them, "Watch out! Be on your guard against all kinds of greed; a man's life does not consist in the abundance of his possessions" (Luke 12:13-15).

When money becomes our top priority, we are admitting by our actions that we believe life *does* consist in the abundance of our possessions.

For years I spent ten and twelve hours a day, sometimes six days a week, building my business. By my actions I was saying I thought life "consisted in the abundance of my possessions"; but I would deny this was the case when my family accused me of being more concerned about the business than I was about them.

I am not saying we don't need money to run our businesses. We obviously do. But the need for money frequently causes us to develop an over-reliance on it. Before we realize it, money has become all-important to our total security. At that point money has become our god—whether we will admit it or not.

Recognizing that all of us have a tendency to place excessive emphasis on money, Jesus gave us a parable about a rich fool:

> And He told them this parable: "The ground of a certain rich man produced a good crop. He thought to himself, 'What shall I do? I have no place to store my crops.' Then he said, 'This is what I'll do. I will tear down my barns and build bigger ones, and there I will store all my grain and my goods. And I'll say to myself, "You have plenty of good things laid up for many years. Take life easy; eat, drink, and be merry." ' But God said to him, 'You fool! This very night your life will be demanded from you. Then who will get what you have prepared for yourself?' This is how it will be with anyone who stores up things for himself but is not rich toward God" (Luke 12:16-21).

Now let's look at this great and powerful parable point by point, principle by principle.

At the outset we see a businessman who has achieved what all of us in business hope for—success. The Lord even points out that his farm "produced a good crop." He was successful. He was getting a very good return on his hard work and investment. Business was so good he outgrew his physical plant.

But then Jesus tells us of his problem: "What shall I do? I have no place to store my crops," he worries. So he decides to expand his physical plant to handle the growth of his business. "This is what I'll do," he says. "I will tear down my barns and build bigger ones, and there I will store all my grain and my goods."

Up to this point, the rich businessman had done nothing wrong. It wasn't wrong to have a good crop. It wasn't wrong to expand his physical plant to handle his burgeoning business. Jesus was not criticizing a healthy, growing business venture.

However, the rich businessman's sin is seen in the fact that he said to himself, "You have plenty of good things laid up for many years. Take life easy; eat, drink, and be merry." There's the problem! This man looked at all his wealth and decided he was self-secure. He could supply all his needs with his wealth for years to come. He was trusting in his wealth and "good things" to supply his needs—instead of God.

As I mentioned earlier, a friend and I once started a small manufacturing business. Our goal was to build the business fast, make it highly profitable, and sell it in a short time. We hoped it would earn enough so that we could retire at a relatively young age.

In other words, we wanted to make enough money so we wouldn't have to trust God to supply any of our future needs. We could trust our money instead.

One day, while reading through the Book of Luke, I ran

across the Parable of the Rich Fool. I had read it many times in the past, but now I felt as though I were reading it for the first time. I realized I was trying to do the same thing as the rich businessman in the parable. I wanted to be able to say, "Myron, you have plenty of good things laid up for many years. You have invested your money wisely. You'll never have another financial worry. So enjoy life to the full, eat, drink, and be merry."

Then I read God's answer to the rich businessman's statement: "But God said to him, 'You fool! This very night your life will be demanded from you. Then who will get what you have prepared for yourself?' " What a strong statement of condemnation from God!

God said the man was a fool to spend his time, energy, and money trying to become totally self-sufficient. Why? Because he could rely on God's wealth to meet all his future needs. He was also a fool for not recognizing that wealth does not provide security for the future. Only God can give us security, because God has control over our lives. God determines whether we live or die—and all the financial wealth in the world can't guarantee life tomorrow.

Finally God indicates that the rich businessman had been a fool for being so selfish with his wealth. He was trying to store up wealth for himself, rather than accumulating "wealth for God."

When I read those verses I realized that I, like the rich businessman, had been deceived into believing that money and wealth were the way to security for the future. As that parable points out, anyone who is more concerned about amassing wealth for himself than about storing up treasures in heaven is deceived and a fool.

Your Loyalty Is Where Your Wealth Is

Jerry Marshall and I started Sunlight Industries, a solar equipment manufacturing company, with very little money. We started off in a small room approximately 20' x 20'. Our only equipment consisted of a few small hand tools and a couple of old, worn-out workbenches we borrowed from a friend.

Both Jerry and I were involved with other businesses at the time, and for a few months we were more committed to them than to Sunlight Industries. After all, we received most of our incomes from those other sources.

But as Sunlight Industries grew from a small room with used workbenches to a full-blown factory with over fifty people on the payroll, our loyalties shifted from our other business interests to Sunlight Industries. Why? Because that is where our time, energy, money, and other resources were being invested.

What started out to be a part-time venture turned into a full-time business. Within a few months we were totally involved in the planning and further development of our manufacturing operation. And the more of our time, energy, and money we devoted to Sunlight Industries, the more loyal and committed we were to it.

This type of loyalty is exactly what Jesus was talking about when He said:

> Do not store up for yourselves treasures on earth, where moth and rust destroy, and where thieves break in and steal. But store up for yourselves treasures in heaven, where moth and rust do not destroy, and where thieves do not break in and steal. For where your treasure is, there your heart will be also (Matt. 6:19-21).

Our hearts always follow our treasures. Notice Jesus didn't say, "Where your heart is, there your treasure will be also." He said just the opposite: "Where your treasure is, *there* your heart will be."

Most business people are highly committed to their businesses because that is where their treasure is. That is, their businesses are their most valuable possessions; therefore, they do not have a problem making sacrifices or commitments to see that the businesses succeed.

These are very difficult verses for business people to deal with. The very nature of business requires us to accumulate a certain amount of wealth, material value, or "treasure." If we didn't, it would be very hard to stay in business.

Yet a failure to understand verses like these has caused numerous Christian business people to make the same rationalization I made as an eight-year-old trying to sell worms: "God is only interested in religious stuff. Since business isn't religious stuff, God certainly couldn't be interested in business." We then take this rationalization (which is really a deception promoted by Satan) a step further. We say, "These verses don't apply to me and my business today. They may have applied back in Bible times, but not in today's rapid-paced business community."

Let's look closely at what Jesus is saying in these verses in Matthew, as a very important principle is contained here. Christ is indicating that even if you devote your whole life to laying up treasures on earth, you *still* don't have real security; for as *The Living Bible* puts it, such goods "can erode away or may be stolen" (Matt 6:19, TLB).

A friend of mine spent fifteen years working overseas so that he could save enough money to buy his own business.

He and his wife came back to the United States with $400,000 in savings. He invested the money in a business—but disaster struck. Within two years he declared bankruptcy. Market conditions had changed and there was no longer a need for his product.

My friend had worked hard. He had saved every cent he could. But at the time he bought his business he had no way of knowing that new technology would make his services obsolete.

In Matthew, Jesus says it is much more profitable—in light of eternity—to put your efforts into the kingdom of God. The efforts or "treasures" placed there are totally safe; God Himself protects them. A drop in the price of stocks or gold, new technology, economic depressions, political takeovers, or a host of other factors can't cause you to lose what you've invested in God's kingdom. But any of the things I've just listed can destroy your "treasure" on earth.

It's also worth noting—as Jesus pointed out in the Parable of the Rich Fool—that even if nothing happens to destroy our treasure on earth, when we die it is all left behind for someone else to enjoy. But when we invest our treasures in the kingdom of God, we can collect on our investment throughout all eternity. I don't know of a brokerage firm anywhere that can even come *close* to matching that kind of return on investment!

Jesus was teaching us one other principle through the passage in Matthew. As you recall, He said, "For where your treasure is, there your heart will be also" (Matt. 6:21). This is a very important principle. Our Lord was telling us that we become committed and loyal to the things in which we invest our resources. If we invest *all* our resources in our businesses, we'll have very little commitment to God and His kingdom—because our loyalties already will be committed to our businesses. On the other hand, if we lay up treasures in heaven, our commitment will be to God. It isn't difficult to let God be Lord of our lives when we have committed everything we have to Him.

Every Christian business person must deal personally with Jesus Christ's statements in Matthew 6:19-21. I can't ignore them. To ignore them is to say I have decided to store up treasures on earth, to make business more important than God and His kingdom. To ignore Jesus Christ's statements in this passage is to say I am more committed to the storing up of wealth on earth than I am to God and His kingdom. The question is, "How do I lay up treasures in heaven?" If that's what I must do, I must know *how* to do it. We will deal with this issue in detail in a later chapter.

The Christian Business Person's Responsibility with Money

As we noted earlier, the Bible never says that money is bad. However, it does say "the love of money is a root of all kinds of evil" (1 Tim. 6:10). Please notice that this verse says the *love* of money is the cause of all kinds of evil—not money itself. And as Deuteronomy states, "Always remember that it is the Lord your God who gives you power to become rich, and He does it to fulfill His promise to your ancestors" (Deut. 8:18, TLB).

In short, God is not against wealth. He gives His people the power to acquire wealth. He is, however, strongly against us loving money more than we love Him. And he expects us to realize that with money comes great responsibility. The Apostle Paul instructed Timothy to:

> Tell those who are rich not to be proud and not to trust in their money, which will soon be gone, but their pride and trust should be in the living God who always richly gives us all we need for our enjoyment (1 Tim. 6:17, TLB).

This verse tells the Christian business person four important things about money.

First, if you have money, you are not to be proud that you have it. Nor should you think you are better, or more favored by God, than those who don't.

Second, you are not to put your faith in your money—as we have seen in both Luke 12 and Matthew 6:19-21.

Third, our pride and trust are to be in God, because He is the One who gives us everything we need to enjoy life.

And fourth, God intends for us to enjoy life with the money He supplies.

But our responsibilities do not end there. Paul goes on to outline what God wants us to do with the money He gives us:

> Tell them to use their money to do good. They should be rich in good works and should give happily to those in need, always being ready to share with others whatever God has given them (1 Tim. 6:18, TLB).

God gives us wealth so that we can share it with others who have a financial need. And not only are we to give to those in need, but we "should give happily" to such individuals. We should *enjoy* using the money God provides us to serve the needs of others. That's why He gave it to us in the first place.

Paul concludes this passage by describing what will happen if we apply these principles: "By doing this they will be storing up real treasure for themselves in heaven—it is the only safe investment for eternity! And they will be living a fruitful Christian life down here as well" (1 Tim. 6:19, TLB).

In effect God is telling us that one way to store up treasures in heaven is by sharing our treasures here on earth with those in need. Rather than making a deposit in an earthly bank, we should make a deposit with needy people. It is this type of deposit that gets credited to our account in God's heavenly bank. And it is the only safe investment we can make, because it is an investment in eternity!

Finally, the verse says that by using our wealth to serve the needs of others we will be "living a fruitful Christian life down here as well." In other words, a fruitful life is not aqchieved by laying up treasures for our own security. The real way to attain security for the future, and to enjoy a fruitful life, is to use the riches God gives us to help meet the needs of others.

As we are faithful in applying these biblical truths and sharing what we have to assist other people, we will reap the reward promised in Luke:

> For if you give, you will get! Your gift will return to you in full and overflowing measure, pressed down, shaken together to make room for more, and running over. Whatever measure you use to give—large or small—will be used to measure what is given back to you (Luke 6:38, TLB).

Isn't that fantastic? God gives us wealth so we can use it to help those in need. Then, as we are faithful in using our wealth in the way He intends, He gives us even more! Why? So we can continue to apply 1 Timothy 6:18 and meet the needs of still more people. As we do that, we continue to reap the rewards stated in Luke 6:38. The end result is that we can never outgive God!

God says, "For if you give, you will get! Your gift will return to you in full and overflowing measure." God tells us that real security—both in this life and for eternity—comes when we obey Him and give to others as He has given to us. And that, my dear friend, is the best business deal around!

Chapter Summary

In this chapter we have looked at why people go into business. The main reason people do so is to make money. We also evaluate how well a business is doing by how much money it makes.

Money becomes the controlling force in most businesses. We tend to make our business decisions in terms of whether they will make or save money. Therefore, money frequently winds up controlling us—even though we don't like to admit it.

Later in the chapter we looked at the source of money and wealth. The Bible indicates that two sources of wealth exist—God and Satan. God promises to give His people the power they need to get wealth; yet Satan also tells people he can give them power and wealth.

Since money plays such an important role in the life of any business, it frequently traps us. We come to believe that money represents security; therefore, the more money we have, the more secure we are.

Money also traps us when we put our faith in it instead of God. *If money can meet my needs,* we figure, *why trust God?*

Yet the Parable of the Rich Fool in Luke 12 demonstrates the shortcomings of trusting money rather than God. It is futile to spend our lives trying to acquire security through wealth when God could take our lives tonight and our wealth would go to someone else.

In this chapter we also saw that one's loyalties and commitments reside where one's "treasure" is (Matt. 6:19-21). Jesus instructed us to lay up treasures in heaven because they are never secure on earth.

And finally, we saw in 1 Timothy 6:19 that a way to lay up treasures in heaven is to share the riches God gives us with people who have a need. And according to Luke 6:38, as we share our riches with those in need, God will give us back more than we gave!

Personal Application

1. Study Luke 12:16-21.
    a. How have your life and business been like those of the man in this parable? How have they been different?
    b. What principles is God teaching you in this parable? How can you apply them to your life and business?

2. Study Matthew 6:19-21.
    a. How do our treasures on earth tend to erode?
    b. In your opinion, how much security does wealth give you?
    c. What do you think it means to "Lay up treasures in heaven"?
    d. Why do we often find it hard to apply Matthew 6:20?
    e. Where have you been laying up your treasures?

3. Study 1 Timothy 6:10, 17-19.
    a. Why is the love of money the cause of evil?
    b. Have you ever experienced negative results from loving

or excessively pursuing money?
c. Why does having money often make us proud?
d. Pray and ask God to show you someone with a financial need you can meet.
e. Keep track of how God blesses you for fulfilling the command outlined in D.
f. Begin sharing with another business person the things God teaches you as you read and study this book.

3
You Can't Serve
Two Masters

Recently, while having lunch in the coffee shop of Denver's Stapleton International Airport, I saw a longtime friend and business acquaintance, Ted Baxter. Ted was sitting alone at a table on the other side of the room, so I picked up my sandwich and cup of coffee and joined him. "Myron," he said as I sat down, "I was just thinking about you."

Ted told me he had just finished reading one of my books. "You know, Myron," he said, "if a person isn't careful, he can carry this thing of mixing religion and business too far." He took a sip of his coffee, then continued. "The way I see it, business is business and church is church and the two don't mix too well. Where I go to church, the people aren't too interested in my business. And where I do business, people aren't too interested in my church."

Ted and I had discussed this issue before and I had learned from experience that it was usually better to just sit back and let him finish saying what was on his mind. I quickly recognized that this was going to be one of those times.

"I think I'm as good a Christian as the next fella," he continued. "I'm chairman of the finance committee at church, my kids sing in the choir, and my wife Marge is always inviting visitors over for lunch on Sunday. Why, I even helped build our church five years ago," he declared, seemingly trying to reassure himself of his fine Christian standing.

"But I have to admit," he said as he finished his coffee, "I guess I *am* a hard-nosed businessman. I don't run a welfare program or mission. I run a business. Don't get me wrong," he said, trying to cut a tough slice of roast beef with a dull knife, "I ask God to help me run my business. When your payroll is as big as mine, you'd better be getting some help from somewhere. It takes a lot of money to keep a business like mine going these days."

As I left Ted in the coffee shop and ran off to catch my flight, I felt extremely frustrated. I've known Ted Baxter a long time. He's a fine gentleman, loves his church, and is a respected businessman in the community. Like so many other Christian business people, however, he believes in the "separation of God and business." As he said, "Business is business and church is church."

That's a very convenient position. Such a philosophy allows us to divide our lives into "sections." It encourages us to categorize life according to our "business life," "home life," "religious or church life," and so on. It also allows us to adopt the premise that what we do in one area of our lives has no consequence in any of the others.

It also permits us to possess many "gods." We can have our religious god, our business god, our pleasure god, etc. Of course, very few people in this country actually place little tin gods in the corners of their living rooms and worship them. We are much too "advanced" and "sophisticated" to do that. Instead, we print our gods on green paper, spend most of our lives trying to collect as many of them as we can, and store them in religious shrines called banks.

Getting Our Priorities Straight

As we saw in chapter 2, making money is the top priority of most people in business. And I must confess that for years it was *my* top priority. I started five businesses for the sole purpose of making money.

That's why this chapter focuses on how to put God first in your business. It will concentrate on how to make Him Lord of your business—as well as Lord of the rest of your life.

If God is going to have first place in your business, He has to *be* first. For example, if God is first in your business, then money can't be. As Jesus said, "No one can serve two masters. Either he will hate the one and love the other, or he will be devoted to the one and despise the other. You cannot serve both God and money" (Matt. 6:24).

This verse points out that two masters exist in this world, and that we will serve one or the other—but we can't serve *both*. These two masters are diametrically opposed. And as the verse so clearly states, if we love one, we will hate the other.

This passage also tells us that we must choose between the two masters—God or money. There you have it! We have a choice to make. Either we will serve God (and He will be the Master and Lord of our business), or we will serve money (and it will become the master and lord of our business). Every business person must choose one or the other.

Most business people, including Christians, have chosen money to be their lord in the marketplace; that is, they have allowed money to become the top priority and controlling factor in all their business decisions. As mentioned in chapter 2, money becomes their security. Their faith is in their money and in its ability to meet all their needs.

God, however, wants to be the true Lord of your business and marketplace. He wants to be your top priority, the controlling factor in all your business decisions. He wants to be your security. And He wants you to put your faith in Him to meet all your needs. But for God to be first in your business, money cannot occupy that position.

The Results of Serving Money

I recently heard a very wealthy Christian businessman speak on the subject of "success." We'll call him Bill.

Bill started out as a used car salesman. Through hard work, diligence, and wise investments, he became a multi-millionaire at a young age. He now speaks to groups all over the country on how to attain success.

During his talk Bill said, "When I started out, my goal was to make $1,000 a month. When I achieved that, I set a goal of $25,000 a year. Once I made that, I raised the goal to $50,000, then $100,000 a year."

As he paced back and forth across the stage he talked faster and faster. Waving his arms he cried, "Today I am a multimillionaire! But it isn't enough! I will never be satisfied with the amount of money I make. When I reach one goal, I always want more, because I can always think of bigger things I want to spend it on. And if you want to be successful, you must never be satisfied with what you've got!"

Bill is a classic example of what Solomon spoke of in Ecclesiastes:

He who loves money shall never have enough. The foolishness of thinking that wealth brings happiness! The more you have, the more you spend, right up to the limits of your income, so what is the advantage of wealth—except perhaps to watch it as it runs through your fingers (Ecc. 5:10-11, TLB).

As this passage reveals, the result of serving money is that we are never satisfied. Our happiness is in the things money can buy us; therefore, we must always buy more and more and bigger and bigger "things." That's the only way we'll stay happy.

Yet Jesus warned: "Watch out! Be on your guard against all kinds of greed; a man's life does not consist in the abundance of his possessions" (Luke 12:15).

Indeed, when money is our lord, we're doomed to unhappiness. Why? Because we never have enough. Because we're always worried about losing what we have. As Solomon so deftly observed, "The abundance of a rich man permits him no sleep" (Ecc. 5:12).

Also, when we allow ourselves to serve money we tend to forget about God; we give *ourselves* the credit for our accomplishments. Notice what Deuteronomy says:

When you have eaten and are satisfied ... be careful that you do not forget the Lord your God, failing to observe His commands ... otherwise, when you eat and are satisfied, when you build fine houses and settle down, and when your herds and flocks grow large and your silver and gold increase and all

you have is multiplied, then your heart will become
proud and you will forget the Lord your God . . . you
may say to yourself, "My power and the strength of
my hands have produced this wealth for me." But
remember the Lord your God, for it is He who gives
you the ability to produce wealth (8:10-18).

Finally, when money is the lord of our marketplace, it
becomes very difficult to enter God's kingdom. This is vividly
described in Matthew 19:16-24.

In this passage a man came to Jesus, asking how to have
eternal life. When Jesus told him to obey the commandments, the man replied, "All these I have kept. . . . What do I
still lack?" (Matt. 19:20) Jesus immediately replied, "If you
want to be perfect, go, sell your possessions and give to the
poor, and you will have treasure in heaven. Then come, follow
Me" (19:21).

But when the young man heard this, "He went away sad,
because he had great wealth" (19:22). His wealth had become more important to him than serving God.

The passage ends with Jesus making a powerful statement
concerning the dangers of trusting in money and wealth:

I tell you the truth, it is hard for a rich man to enter
the kingdom of heaven. Again I tell you, it is easier
for a camel to go through the eye of a needle than
for a rich man to enter the kingdom of God (19:23-
24).

The "eye of the needle" was a small gate located in the wall
surrounding Jerusalem. To go through the gate, a camel had
to get down on its knees and any cargo it was carrying had to
be unloaded. Only then could the animal slowly crawl through
the Eye of the Needle.

Thus, Jesus was saying it is as difficult for a rich person to enter heaven as it is for a camel to go through that gate. For like the camel, the rich person must be willing to humble himself and give up his "cargo" of riches; he must make God, rather than wealth, his Master and Lord.

The Results of Putting God First in your Business

Earlier we saw that Jesus said men could not serve both God and money (Matt. 6:24). It is interesting to note that in the same passage He also said, "Therefore I tell you, do not worry about your life, what you will eat or drink; or about your body, what you will wear" (Matt. 6:25).

Isn't that amazing? Jesus said that we can't simultaneously serve God and money. And yet, we have no need to worry about our lives and all our material needs. What irony! People make money the top priority in their lives because they are worried about their material needs. And they think having money is the way to insure that those needs are met.

But Jesus is saying here that if we serve God instead of money, we won't need to worry about such things. Isn't this concept the very opposite of what we generally believe, at least in practice?

Four times in this passage Jesus assures us that if we've put God first in our lives, we won't need to worry about material possessions:

Who of you by worrying can add a single hour to his life? (Matt. 6:27)

And why do you worry about clothes? (6:27)

So do not worry saying, "What shall we eat?" or

"What shall we drink?" or "What shall we wear?"
(Matt. 6:31)
For the pagans run after all these things, and your
Heavenly Father knows that you need them (6:32).

Did you catch that? Jesus is saying that we aren't to worry
about these things—things that people think they'll get if
money is first in their lives. God already knows exactly what
we need!

Remember my friend Ted Baxter, the guy who said, "The
way I see it, business is business and church is church"? He
wasn't in favor of mixing religion and business. Do you
remember how concerned he was about meeting payroll?
Guess what? Through the statements listed above, Jesus is
demonstrating that God knows what businessmen worry
about. He knows what it takes to run a business. And not only
does He *know*, He *promises* that if we make Him Lord and
Master of our business, He will supply everything we need.

Finally, Jesus instructs us to "seek first His kingdom and
His righteousness, and all these things will be given to you as
well" (Matt. 6:33). What things will be given to us? All the
things the pagans run after by making money their master!
And how do we get these things? By putting God, instead of
money, first in our businesses.

Thus we see that God is saying to all business people, "You
have a choice. You can serve Me or money, but you can't
serve us both. Therefore, you must choose between us.

"If you choose Me, you won't need to worry about your
business needs being met; as long as you are putting Me and
My kingdom first, I'll supply you with all the things other
business people are trying to get by putting money first."

The key to true business success, therefore, is making *God* the Lord of our marketplace. That is, we are to seek His kingdom and righteousness first in our businesses and lives.

Satan deceives the vast majority of business people into thinking that the way to succeed in business is to make money; therefore, money has become their master. To them, "good business sense" is simply doing those things that make the most money. And on the surface, this seems like a logical way to operate a business. *Besides, we think, it must be the right way to do business; that's the way everyone does it.*

Yet God tells us that though our ways seem right to us, and appear logical, they usually are woefully misguided (Prov. 14:12). In fact, He says that man's thoughts and ways are fundamentally different from His thoughts and ways (Isa. 55:8). This means that we must take God's Word and obey it—even if it seems to contradict the world's formulas for success. When we do, we'll be pleasantly surprised.

Kenny Hughes is a bush pilot who also operates a repair shop near Big Lake, Alaska. "Not long ago I needed $3,500 and I didn't have it," he told me. "I guess I could have gone to the bank and borrowed the money like most people. But instead, I prayed and told God I wasn't going to borrow the money. If He wanted me to have the $3,500, He could supply it some way other than me borrowing it."

He smiled and said, "The next day an insurance company called and offered to sell me a crashed Cessna 206 airplane for $1,500. I took them up on their offer, picked up the phone, and called some friends I knew who needed Cessna parts. I sold the engine alone for $6,500!"

Kenny was beaming as he finished his story. "You know, I could have taken things into my own hands and borrowed the money. But by trusting God to meet the needs in my business, He not only supplied the $3,500 I needed, but a whole lot more!"

Kenny Hughes' story is a classic example of how we can prove that biblical principles work on a practical basis in our businesses. And not only do they work, but they work far better than the world's ways!

It's Your Move

I don't know you. I don't know where you are in your growth as a Christian, I don't even know if you *are* a Christian. Nor do I know the type of business you're in—whether you are an owner or an employee. But I do know one thing. God's Word is true. And when God says He knows our needs and will supply them all—if we put Him first over money—we can be sure of one thing: we're hearing the truth.

I have proven this fact in my own businesses. I have met numerous other business people who also have proven it. And you can prove it too.

It won't necessarily be easy. In fact, it may be the hardest thing you've ever done in your life. The world's philosophy has a tight hold on most of us; we usually find it difficult to swim upstream against the tide of popular public opinion. But numerous Christian business people out in the marketplace can speak from experience that it is well worth the effort.

Before you continue to the next chapter, I'd like to challenge you to make a commitment to God—if you haven't done so already. Allow Him to be the Lord and Master in your business. To do this, let me offer a simple suggestion. Start by making a list of your assets and liabilities. These liabilities represent the needs that God has said He will meet if you make Him Lord and seek His will.

Next, pray over each asset and liability and tell God you will use these assets as He directs. Reaffirm that you are trusting Him—not the bank—to meet your liabilities, and that you will diligently follow His instructions in meeting those obligations.

Finally, thank Him for becoming the Lord of your marketplace and daily reaffirm your commitment to Him.

Chapter Summary

Many people believe God and business just don't mix. They tend to agree with my friend, Ted Baxter, when he said, "Business is business and church is church." But God not only *wants* to be involved in every Christian's business, He *expects* to be.

For God to be first in our businesses, He must become more important to us than money. As we saw in Matthew: "You cannot serve both God and money" (6:24). We must choose one or the other; we can't serve both.

If we choose to serve money, we will never be satisfied. As Ecclesiastes points out, "Whoever loves money never has money enough" (5:10).

Further, when money is our master, we tend to forget about God and are deceived into believing it was our own shrewd business ability that produced our success. The Book of Deuteronomy confirms this fact: "Then your heart will become proud and you will forget the Lord your God...you may say to yourself, 'My power and the strength of my hands have produced this wealth for me'" (8:14,17).

If we make God Master and Lord, however, He promises we won't have to worry about our financial needs being met. Jesus challenged us over this very point (Matt. 6:25-34). He also assured us that He knew what our needs were, and that He would meet all of them if we put God first—instead of money.

Personal Application

1. Read Matthew 6:24. Why do you think Jesus said, "You cannot serve both God and money"?

2. Read Matthew 6:25-34 and pick out all the times Jesus told us not to worry.
   a. What are the things you are worrying about in your business right now?
   b. What is the source of those worries?
   c. Commit the issue to God and ask Him to help you stop worrying about it.

3. Read Matthew 6:32-33.
   a. What needs do you currently have in your business? (Make a list of them).
   b. Start praying daily, asking God to meet those needs and thanking Him for the answers.

4
Putting God First as Your Senior Business Partner

A real estate development company was interested in having me do some consulting work. As we talked, one of the firm's employees said, "Before we make a decision, we will have to discuss this with our senior partner, George Bunting. Mr. Bunting owns the controlling interest in our firm. We wouldn't want to do anything without his input and approval."

As I left their office, I was reminded of the fact that *God* is to be the Christian's senior business partner. Before we make our business decisions, we should obtain God's input and approval. Yet for some of us that is easier said than done.

The Problem of Control
Business owners, as we've already seen, want to make money. But most have at least one other goal: They also want to be *in charge*. I must admit that, for me, the power of ownership is very appealing. I like the idea of owning "my" business.

Perhaps you are more mature than I am, but for me the term, "my business," has a beautiful ring to it.

I enjoy having the final say, making the decisions, running the risks, and reaping the benefits when "I" succeed. I get great satisfaction out of feeling that "I" am in control.

Furthermore, I often feel that I have a *right* to be in control; after all, I take all the risks. "My" money started the business. "My" time was spent making something out of nothing. "My" ideas solved the problems.

As a result of this type of attitude, many business people find it difficult to commit their businesses to God. Oh, some of them give lip service to the commitment, but when it comes to actually seeking God's will in a business decision or putting God above money, theirs is a hollow commitment.

During a coffee break at a management seminar, Martha Nettles, owner of a travel agency, told me with a smile, "I don't have any trouble turning my business over to God when it's bill paying time. But as soon as I book a few good tours, I'm always ready to take it back." She shrugged her shoulders. "I hate to admit it, but I'm afraid I just try to keep God around to solve my problems, not to really help me run my business the way He wants it to operate."

As we walked back into the meeting room she turned to me and said, "If I'm really truthful, I guess I want to be free to run my business the way I want to. I keep God around to sort of 'rubber stamp' my plans and decisions."

As I walked to the front of the meeting room to start the next session of the seminar, I had to admit to myself that I also was guilty of harboring similar feelings. Instead of asking *God* what I should do, I sometimes would say, "God, here is what *I'm* going to do—now please bless it." Yet all the while, I would try to convince myself that I was obeying God's will for my life and business.

Our "Secular" Life Versus Our "Spiritual" Life

Satan has cleverly deceived many of us into believing that when we become Christians, our lives suddenly are divided into two parts—our "Christian" or spiritual lives, and our "secular" or non-spiritual lives.

If he is successful in convincing us that we now live two lives—spiritual and secular—his next goal is to try to persuade us that our "spiritual" lives consist of those activities which we participate in at church or in the privacy of our own homes. All of our other pursuits, however—those which are conducted out in the marketplace—are "secular" and have no spiritual significance. Thus, if we say that Jesus Christ is "Lord" of our lives, we're referring only to our "spiritual" lives. We are still perfectly free to retain control over our "secular" or business lives.

This view, however, is clearly at odds with what the Lord wants for us. The Bible never mentions our "spiritual" lives and our "secular" lives. When we accept Jesus Christ as our Saviour and Lord, He becomes Lord of *every* area of our lives—both in *and* out of the marketplace.

What Happens When God Becomes "Lord" of Our Lives

The *Funk and Wagnalls* dictionary defines a lord as "one possessing supreme power and authority." If Jesus Christ becomes Lord of our lives, it means that He possesses supreme power and authority over us. We become His "servants." The same dictionary defines a servant as "a slave or bondsman."

Paul similarly tells us, "But now that you have been set free from sin and have become slaves to God, the benefit you reap leads to holiness, and the result is eternal life" (Rom. 6:22). Likewise, in 1 Corinthians he says:

Haven't you yet learned that your body is the home of the Holy Spirit God gave you, and that He lives within you? Your own body does not belong to you. For God has bought you with a great price. So use every part of your body to give glory back to God, because He owns it (6:19-20, TLB).

Notice that this latter passage points out that God has "bought us with a great price." He actually owns us! We are His—lock, stock, and barrel. Notice also that the verse claims that God owns *every part* of our bodies.

I used to think that the phrase, "We have been bought with a price," was referring to our salvation—that Jesus Christ's death on the cross had paid for our eternal life.

I wanted to believe the eternal life part, but I wasn't so sure I wanted to accept the idea that He was "Lord of my life." Yet this passage in 1 Corinthians clearly indicates that God did not just buy our eternal life—He bought *us*. It says that *every* part of our bodies belongs to God.

Now, let me ask you a question: If as a Christian I am owned by God, and as a business person I have a business, then who owns the business? If your answer was, "God," you're right. If God owns us, then everything we have belongs to Him.

Paul describes the implications of this relationship in Philippians:

But whatever was to my profit I now consider loss for the sake of Christ. What is more, I consider everything a loss compared to the surpassing greatness of knowing Christ Jesus my Lord, for whose sake I have lost all things. I consider them rubbish, that I may gain Christ (3:7-8).

Paul clearly understood what it meant to make Jesus Christ Lord of his life. He realized that since God had purchased him through Jesus' death on the cross, everything he owned belonged to God. Notice again what the apostle said: "I consider everything *a loss* compared to the surpassing greatness of knowing Christ Jesus my Lord, for whose sake I have lost all things. I consider them *rubbish,* that I may gain Christ."

Paul was saying that it was well worth it to accept Christ and receive eternal life in return. For when he gave himself to God, he was no longer the owner of his tentmaking business—God was. Moreover, he considered his business "rubbish" compared to gaining Christ as his personal Saviour. In essence, Jesus had become Paul's senior partner. He owned the controlling interest in everything Paul had.

When you accept Jesus Christ as personal Saviour and Lord of your life, like Paul, God owns you. And if He owns you, He owns your business as well. God becomes your senior business partner with the controlling interest in all you possess.

What Happens When God Becomes Our Senior Partner

As I said earlier, most business owners and managers like to be "in control." Therefore, it isn't always easy for us to accept Christ as Lord and to turn our businesses over to Him. If we do, we're afraid we'll lose our precious control.

I remember struggling with this issue in my own life. I had

worked hard to get my business going. I had built its reputation and feared that if I allowed God to take control, He might decide to do something with it that was contrary to my wishes. He might even tell me to do something else with my life!

Because of those fears, it took me a long time to come to the point where I could say, "OK, God. You're my senior partner. I give You controlling interest in my business."

One of the verses that ultimately helped me to make that decision is in Jeremiah: "'For I know the plans I have for you,' declares the Lord, 'plans to prosper you and not to harm you, plans to give you hope and a future'" (29:11). I also discovered Job 22:21: "Submit to God and be at peace with Him; in this way prosperity will come to you."

In these verses, God is saying that He has a plan for us; specifically, He will prosper us if we submit to Him, and live in peace with Him and ourselves. This promise, moreover, is not limited solely to our businesses. He will prosper us in *every* area of our lives—including our homes, our relationships, our quality of life, etc. All we need to do is submit to Him!

And importantly, by yielding to God, we're not "losing control." On the contrary: God is helping us to get all aspects of our lives *under control.* We're not giving up a business, we're gaining a partner—a partner who says, "I will instruct you . . . and guide you along the best pathway for your life; I will advise you and watch your progress" (Ps. 32:8, TLB).

That doesn't sound like a business partner who takes anything away from us; it sounds like someone who is totally committed to helping us, teaching us, and advising us so we can experience the best possible success!

I don't know about you, but I need that kind of help in running my business. I don't know of a consultant anywhere who could do for your business what God promises to do! And believe me, He's proven Himself a trustworthy senior partner time and time again.

A few years ago my former business partner and I were looking for a vice-president of marketing for Sunlight Industries, our manufacturing firm. With our limited skills in sales and marketing, we felt that we had taken the company just about as far as we could. Now we needed an expert in this field to "come on board."

So we began seeking advice from people who ran companies bigger than our own. We asked them how they went about finding their marketing people. Some told us that we should use professional "headhunters"—people who are paid a fee to find business executives. Others said that we should advertise in the leading newspapers and trade journals. It seemed that everyone had a different opinion to offer us.

Our search was further complicated by the fact that we wanted our future vice-president to be a Christian. Apart from his experience in marketing, sales, and management, we wanted him to be committed to the same biblical principles of management and business that we were.

As I thought about the type of person we were looking for, I was certain we would never find an individual with the right qualifications. I also was acutely aware that federal discrimination laws would never permit us to advertise for a distinctly Christian co-worker. At this point, I had just about reached the edge of despair.

Finally we opted to run an ad in *The Wall Street Journal*; I began preparing the job description. But one evening Jerry, my partner, came over to my house. "I really feel we should commit the problem of finding a marketing man to God," he said. "Let Him provide the person He wants."

I wasn't so sure that God was running an employment agency on the side, but I agreed with Jerry. We decided to pray and ask God to help us find the right person. We spent the evening praying, telling God about the kind of person we felt we needed. We mentioned how important it was for him to be highly qualified in the field of sales and marketing, and we stressed that we wanted a person who also would be a strong Christian, someone who'd want to apply biblical principles in business.

Several days later I flew to Seattle to run a management seminar. My wife flew up to meet me the following day. As I picked her up at the airport she handed me a note. "I met the most interesting people on the plane," she remarked. "They were from Colorado Springs [our hometown] too. When I told them about your business, and that you were looking for a marketing and sales manager, they gave me the name of a man who's just moved to Colorado Springs from Texas. His name's Jim Ander. They said he had lots of experience in marketing."

I put her note in my pocket and forgot about it until after the seminar. But when I returned home, I found the note, called Jim, and set up an appointment to meet him.

During the course of our conversation, I learned that Jim had worked with Zig Ziglar and had been the number-one salesperson for Sales Masters. He had extensive experience in international marketing, was a fine Christian committed to running a business on scriptural principles, and to top it off, he lived right in Colorado Springs!

I couldn't believe it. We had been ready to spend thousands of dollars trying to recruit, hire, and relocate a marketing director because our business associates told us that was the way to do it. But when we prayed and asked God to pick the person *He* wanted, we found our new V.P. living right in our own city.

When God picks an employee, you can always be sure that person is exactly who you need. Jim Ander took our little company (with $250,000 in annual sales), and within a year he was selling that much in a single month! And as if that weren't enough, Jim has become one of the best friends a person could ever have.

God taught me an important lesson in that experience. When you turn a situation over to the Lord, and then get out of His way, He always works things out better than you could on your own. But I'm not really surprised. For as God promised in Psalm 32:8, He will instruct us and guide us along the best pathway for our businesses. He certainly proved that when He brought us Jim Ander.

I'm still learning a lot, though, about living out these truths on a day-by-day basis. In Luke, Jesus said: "Anyone who wants to follow Me must put aside his own desires and conveniences and carry his cross with him every day and keep close to Me!" (9:23, TLB)

In this verse, the Lord is saying that with every decision, I must choose whether I will make it on my own or seek God's input. I must decide who has veto power: me or God. And even though God *wants* to be my senior business partner with the controlling interest in my life, He never uses His power to lord it over me.

As we saw in Jeremiah 29:11 and Psalm 32:8, God only wants the very best for us. Our job, therefore, is to claim His promises, and trust Him to act in our best interests.

How Involved Will God Get in Your Business?

When Jerry and I first considered what type of person we
wanted God to supply as our V.P. of marketing, I had some
reservations. I wondered just how specific we could get with
God. I knew God was concerned about our needs, but some
of the things on our list seemed to border on plain personal
preference and desire.

As I discussed this with Jerry, he reminded me what God
had promised in the Psalms:

> Be delighted with the Lord. Then He will give you all
> your heart's desires. Commit everything you do to
> the Lord. Trust Him to help you do it and He will"
> (37:4-5, TLB).

These verses point out that God is not only interested in
meeting our basic needs (such as the need for an employee),
but that He also is concerned about our desires (such as the
specific qualifications of that employee).

Sometimes I think we get caught in the mental trap of
believing that God is interested only in our "generic" needs—
such as food, shelter, and clothing. Yet Psalm 37:4 makes it
clear He also will give us our desires as long as we are first
taking delight in Him; that is, as long as we are putting Him
first.

Jerry and I could have prayed for a generic V.P.—and that is
what we would have gotten. However, God wants us to be
specific. He wants to get involved in the "details" of the
company.

In the past few years, I have been learning that God will get
as involved in your business as you ask Him to be. Or, He will
stay as *un*involved as you want. The choice is up to you. As
Jesus Himself said:

Ask, and you will be given what you ask for. Seek, and you will find. Knock, and the door will be opened. For everyone who asks, receives. Anyone who seeks, finds. If only you will knock, the door will open. If a child asks his father for a loaf of bread, will he be given a stone instead? If he asks for fish, will he be given a poisonous snake? Of course not! And if you hardhearted, sinful men know how to give good gifts to your children, won't your Father in heaven even more certainly give good gifts to those who ask Him for them? (Matt. 7:7-11, TLB)

I often wonder how much unnecessary work I create for myself, how many needless expenses I incur, and how often I miss good deals, simply because I don't incorporate the truths of these verses into my life and business.

Actually, I think this passage should be framed and placed on every business person's desk. We all waste time, energy, and money because we don't allow God to get more involved in the details of our lives and businesses!

God never forces Himself on us. Unlike many business people, He will never take charge where He is not welcome. He never infringes on other people's areas of authority. However, when His help is needed, He is always available. When you present a problem to Him, He always has the right answer. And no problem is too large or too small for His attention.

A Personal Challenge

In chapter 3 I challenged you to make a commitment. I asked you to let God rather than money be the Lord of your life and business. I now would challenge you to personally install Him as your senior partner—a partner with the controlling interest in your business. By that I mean you will make a commitment to seeking God's input in your decision-making process. You will seek His will over your own. As you make plans, you will ask God to direct the development of those plans.

If God is your senior partner, you will respect His judgment, input, and opinions. When you ask for His help and He gives you the potential answer or solution, you won't reject it; you will thank Him for it and act on it.

As you do this you will begin to experience the real meaning of success in business. You will discover a fulfillment in your life and business activities that you've never known. And as you make God Lord of your business, you will begin to discover that God has plans and purposes for your business that surpass your wildest dreams.

Chapter Summary
In this chapter we have focused on installing God as your senior business partner. Most of us in business, however, tend to have problems letting go of the power, control, and authority we enjoy as business owners or managers.

We usually think we have a "right" to run our own companies because we are the ones taking all the risks; we're spending our time, energy, and money to make sure our businesses succeed.

As Christian business people, we need to realize that we owe God the place of senior business partner. He should hold the controlling interest in our businesses. First Corinthians states that God has bought us with a price. He has purchased us, and our bodies now belong to Him—not us (6:19-20). Therefore, if He owns us, He also owns all we have. He becomes the "parent company," controlling all we have and do.

When we invite God to be our senior business partner, He promises to instruct and guide us along the best path for our lives and businesses. He also promises to advise us and watch our progress (Ps. 32:8). God wants to get personally involved in both the large and small areas of our businesses. He doesn't want to be a figurehead. He doesn't want us to pray simply, "bless the business"; He wants to be involved in everyday planning and decision-making.

God will get as involved in your business as you want Him to. But His involvement doesn't begin until He is invited.

Personal Application

1. Read and study 1 Corinthians 6:19-20.
   a. Had you ever considered the fact that God actually owns you when you become a Christian?
   b. How does that fact change your outlook on your personal possessions?
   c. What effect does it have on the way you operate your business? Spend your time? Make your plans? Spend your money?
2. Read Jeremiah 29:11 and Psalm 32:8.
   a. What steps will you take to allow God to be more involved in your business-planning process?
   b. Make a list of plans or problems you currently are working on. Each day, spend time with God discussing what should be done.
3. Reread the Jim Ander story in this chapter. What principles do you see in this story that may help you in allowing God to be your senior business partner?

5
The Marketplace as Your Mission Field

Many years ago, the pastor of the church my family attended took me aside for a little talk. "Myron," he said in hushed, reverential tones, "I think God is calling you to the ministry."

This little pronouncement took me by surprise, to say the least. I had always assumed that entering "the ministry" involved a commitment to work full time in a church, or as a missionary. And frankly, since I had never felt a "calling" to that sort of work, I really couldn't see myself *in the ministry*. Besides, I'd been planning to pursue a career in the business world—which would allow me to support those people who *had* been "called."

Satan's "Immaculate Deception"
As we discussed in an earlier chapter, Satan is the master deceiver. He is not the "red devil" with a pitchfork, tail, and horns as portrayed in mythical stories. The Bible describes

70

him as "the prince of this world," "the god of this age," and "an angel of light."

One of his greatest deceptions has been perpetrated against the Christian community. As briefly discussed in chapter 4, Satan has deceived Christians into believing that we have a *spiritual* or religious life, and a *secular* or non-religious life.

This is not a biblical concept; it is of satanic origin. Nowhere does Scripture refer to a "spiritual" life and a "secular" life. Satan has a very clever reason for wanting the Christian to believe that a spiritual/secular duality exists: Once we accept this notion, it becomes easier for him to deceive us into believing that spiritual "calls" are a prerequisite for Christian service.

You see, most of the Christian community has accepted the idea of the "call." The concept goes like this: God "calls" only a few people into "full-time Christian work." If you are one of the *chosen few* "called" into this type of service, then you can have a "religious" job. You can become a pastor, a missionary, etc. But remember: only a *few* people within Christendom are called into full-time Christian work.

This means that the rest of us (by far the majority of Christians) are *not* "called"; we are free to work in the secular world, where our main concern is to provide financial support to the handful of "full-time Christian workers." But we have no real responsibility to the "ministry," because that is a *spiritual* job to be performed only by those who've received the "call."

What a masterful scheme to render Christians ineffective for God. It creates a multitude of spiritually anemic "spectator Christians" who watch from the sidelines, while a small platoon of believers try to battle Satan for the marketplaces of the world. No wonder Satan is winning the fight!

Satan has sold the Christian community one more deception. He has convinced us that our spiritual lives are a *private* matter, and our secular lives are a *public* matter. How convenient! Once we believe that lie, we fall right into Satan's rationalization trap: Since a person's spiritual or religious life is a private matter, we should not intrude into that area of a person's life. Instead, we should focus on our secular life (since it is our public life) and limit all of our relationships and interactions to *that* area.

Once we fall for Satan's private/public life concept, he is then in a position to make us feel nervous or guilty about discussing spiritual principles and issues with people in the marketplace. Obviously, since the marketplace represents the secular or public part of a person's life, it certainly is no place to talk about such private matters as religion—or so the rationalization goes.

As a result, the marketplace is filled with people looking for answers to their personal questions and problems. And though the Christian in the marketplace has the answers and solutions to these problems, he usually keeps quiet for fear of *offending* someone.

This leaves Satan free to bombard the marketplace with all kinds of false religions, cults, and "isms" which convince honest seekers that Jesus Christ is not the answer to their problems. And so these seekers wind up rejecting Jesus Christ (whom they've never had a chance to meet), and criticizing Christianity (which they've never actually seen in action).

If Satan is winning the battle for the marketplace, it's because we're sitting in the bleachers and on the benches;

Satan has deceived us into thinking that it's not our job to reach the world with the Gospel. We need only to support those who do, those who've received the "call."

I once interviewed a young man named Jason for a job. He had just graduated from a four-year Bible college. As we talked he said, "When I went to Bible college, I thought God was calling me to some type of Christian work, but nothing really opened up when I graduated. I guess that means God doesn't want me in full-time Christian service. So," he concluded "I'm looking for a job in computer science."

When I asked him why he was interested in that particular field, he replied, "A person can make a lot of money and build a secure future. I think there is more opportunity for career advancement there than in any other field."

I sat there stunned at what I was hearing. Here was a young man who had attended *four years* of Bible school. But because he hadn't immediately been offered a job in a church, he concluded he wasn't being *called* into *full-time Christian service*. Therefore, he decided that he was free to pursue a career which would lead to financial security!

Jason is a classic example of how successful Satan has been at weaving his web of deception into the hearts and minds of the Christian community. He has lulled believers into indifference, complacency, and apathy. He has wooed us into believing we have a right to spiritual retirement with an honorable discharge; meanwhile, he and his army of assistants systematically devour the marketplace and those in it.

God's Battle Plan for the Marketplace
God isn't just idly sitting by while Satan methodically marches through the marketplace and conquers the business world.

God has His *own* battle plan for bringing true and lasting success to people.

Isaiah introduces this strategy:

The spirit of the Lord God is upon me, because the Lord has anointed me to bring good news to the suffering and afflicted. He has sent me to comfort the brokenhearted, to announce liberty to captives, and to open the eyes of the blind. He has sent me to tell those who mourn that the time of God's favor to them has come (61:1-2, TLB).

Isaiah states that God had anointed him to bring "good news to the suffering and afflicted . . . to tell those who mourn that the time of God's favor to them has come." That was the job of a priest.

God anointed men to serve as priests so that they could have direct access to Him, and then tell others about the true and living God who loves people and wants to meet their every need.

Isaiah then notes, "You shall be called priests of the Lord, ministers of our God" (61:6, TLB). Did you catch that? He said, "*You* shall be called *priests* of the Lord, *ministers* of our God." That means you and me! That means each of God's people!

The apostles realized this. Peter, for example, in writing his first epistle said, "And now you have become living building-stones for God's use in building His house. What's more, you are His holy priests" (1 Peter 2:5, TLB).

Every Christian is one of God's priests here on earth. That is, as Christians, we have direct access to God—and the Lord has given us the responsibility to teach others His ways.

The Apostle John, writing in Revelation, noted: "[He] has

made us to be a kingdom and priests to serve His God and Father" (1:6).

These verses should have great significance to the Christian. They mean that we are *all* *"called"* to be *spiritual ministers* to people in the marketplace. Satan's attempt to deceive people into believing that God "selectively calls" only a few of His people into "Christian service" is just that—deception! It is one way Satan attempts to stifle the Christian community's effectiveness in sharing the Good News about Jesus Christ to a lost and dying world.

Why God Wants to Be Your Senior Business Partner

In chapter 4 we were challenged to let God be our senior business partner—a partner with the controlling interest in our companies. When we give God "controlling interest" in our businesses, He is free to accomplish His plans, goals, and objectives through us. In other words, God is free to accomplish *His* business through *our* businesses.

Let me ask you a question: Just what *is* God's business? It certainly is not to make money. As the psalmist observed, "The earth is the Lord's and everything in it, the world, and all who live in it" (24:1). In other words, God *already* owns it all! There's nothing else He needs; for He has said: "The silver is Mine and the gold is Mine" (Hag. 2:8).

So what is God's business? Jesus succinctly stated the objective of God's activities in this world: "For the Son of man came to seek and to save what was lost" (Luke 19:10); "The thief comes only to steal and kill and destroy; I have come that they may have life, and have it to the full" (John 10:10).

In these two verses, Jesus makes it very clear that God's business is *people*. His goal is to give love, peace, joy, and eternal life to a self-centered, hateful, frustrated, and dying world.

And just how committed is God to accomplishing His business? That famous verse, John 3:16, tells us that God is so committed to reaching people, that He gave His most prized possession, His Son, to die for our sins.

There's one thing, then, of which we always can be sure. When we let God become our senior business partner, His goal and purpose is to use us and our businesses to reach people with the Gospel.

Remember when we discussed Matthew 6:24 back in chapter 3? That verse told us that we cannot serve both God and money. If God is our senior business partner, and we are committed to Him, then *His* goals become *our* goals.

This means that through our businesses, we are to be personally involved in reaching our peers, associates, and employees with the Gospel. The goal of our businesses is no longer simply to make money.

Rather, we should be seeking God's kingdom and His righteousness.

As we saw in John 10:10, God's goal is to reach people with the Gospel. Therefore, as we seek to use our businesses to reach people in the marketplace with the Good News, and as we begin actively pursuing that goal, God has promised He will provide the monetary support we need to accomplish the goals of our businesses (Matt. 6:32-33).

The Christian Business Person's Importance in the Marketplace

Christian business people are in a unique position. We usually have more contact with non-Christians than most other Christians do. Thus, if we're to reach non-Christians with the Good News of Jesus Christ, we must go where they are—*the marketplace,* the nerve center of any society.

Jesus knew this. That is why He spent relatively little time in the synagogues, temples, or places where religious leaders and other elite spiritual groups hung out. Instead, He spent the bulk of His time in the marketplace—making friends and mingling with the "non-Christian types" of His day.

Luke makes note of this fact in his Gospel:

Dishonest tax collectors and other notorious sinners often came to listen to Jesus' sermons; but this caused complaints from the Jewish religious leaders and the experts on Jewish law because He was associating with such despicable people—even eating with them! (15:1-2, TLB)

The religious leaders of Christ's day criticized Him for spending too much time in the marketplace, for associating with and befriending the non-religious, less acceptable people. When Jesus detected their attitude He said,

If you had a hundred sheep and one of them strayed away and was lost in the wilderness, wouldn't you leave the ninety-nine others to go and search for the lost one until you found it?...Well, in the same way heaven will be happier over one lost sinner who returns to God than over ninety-nine others who haven't strayed away! (Luke 15:3-7, TLB)

One day Jesus was out beside a lake talking to a large crowd of people. As He and the crowd walked along the shore, He met a tax collector named Levi. Soon Levi became one of Jesus' disciples; and because He had meals at Levi's house, Jesus had an opportunity to meet many other tax collectors and sinners. In this way, many of these people also became His disciples.

Jesus' plan has not changed in 2,000 years. He is still looking for people who will meet the lost on familiar ground—the marketplace—and show them how to obtain eternal life.

In many respects, the business community is a closed society of untouchable, affluent *paupers*. Misery, pain, hurt, and suffering are camouflaged behind false fronts of fine homes, expensive cars, nice clothes, and a phony look of "altogetherness."

Yet no one is better qualified than the Christian business person to understand the expectations, disappointments, hopes, and fears of such people. The Christian business person rubs shoulders, eats lunch, attends meetings, and does business with them every day. He has a better opportunity than anyone else to lead the non-Christian business person to Jesus Christ.

As a kingdom of priests, God has anointed us, like Isaiah, to bring good news to the suffering and afflicted, to comfort the brokenhearted, to announce liberty to captives, and to open the eyes of the blind.

Thus we are "called" to our professions as business people—just as pastors are "called" by God to serve their churches. And in at least one respect, *every* believer shares the same "calling": we are "to go into all the world and preach the Good News to everyone, everywhere" (Mark 16:15, TLB). There are two key words in that verse: *Everyone* and *everywhere*.

Some of us perform this responsibility as pastors, some as bankers, some as bricklayers, some as salespeople, some as doctors, some as engineers, some as business owners, and so on. *But the "calling" is always the same to all Christians, all the time, everywhere!* Paul neatly summarized this concept when he told Timothy: "Preach the Word of God urgently at all times, whenever you get the chance, in season and out, when it is convenient and when it is not" (2 Tim. 4:2, TLB). That sounds like a full-time call to me!

Even though I am a business owner by occupation, my "calling" is to share Jesus Christ with my corner of the marketplace, my slice of the world. And according to Paul's instruction to Timothy, I am to look for—and make—opportunities to share the Gospel with people. As a businessman, I can attest to the fact that there are opportunities all around us, every day, for us to witness in the marketplace.

How God Uses You and Your Business in the Marketplace

Many Christians who own a business think they should hire only other Christians. Satan loves it when they do! There's nothing he likes better than to have a bunch of Christians form their own little businesses, hire only Christians, do business only with Christians, and attend only Christian functions and activities. These types of arrangements pose absolutely no threat to Satan's plans to control the marketplace. But God *wants* to use you and your business to reach *non-*Christian employees.

Matthew records Jesus as saying, "Come along with Me and I will show you how to fish for the souls of men!" (4:19, TLB) If we are going to fish for the souls of people, we need to interact with men and women whose souls need to be fished for. It's pretty hard to reach people with the Gospel when everyone you know is a Christian!

We need to use our businesses as vehicles for attracting non-Christians. And what better way than to hire some non-Christian employees? You will be around them every day of the week. They can watch your life and you can pray and trust God to provide you with an opportunity to share the Gospel with them. Remember, God is more interested in having these individuals become Christians than you are. He certainly will make opportunities available for you to share your faith in Christ with them.

A few years ago our firm hired a department manager named Ken Perkins. My two business partners—Jim Ander and Jerry Marshall—and I used to meet in my office early Monday mornings to study the Bible and pray for the business.

One Monday morning Ken came in early while we were sitting around a table with our Bibles open. We'd been discussing some verses in Proverbs that we found relevant to today's business climate.

After apologizing for the intrusion, Ken said, "You know, I'd like to join you guys some time for your little meeting—if you wouldn't mind." We assured him that we'd love to include him, and later in the week I made a point of going to lunch with him.

Ken's inadvertent discovery of our Bible study provided a natural opportunity for me to begin discussing the Word with him. I found out that he occasionally attended church, but didn't really understand what a Christian was or how a person could become one. I asked him if he would be interested in getting together for breakfast and a short Bible study the next morning; he replied that he'd really like that.

The next morning Ken and I met at a local pancake house.

After a quick breakfast, I asked him to look up several verses that describe the plan of salvation. By the time we had finished discussing these verses, Ken was ready to accept Christ.

Soon thereafter, he began attending our church; within a few weeks, he was bringing his assistant manager and some of the employees from his department with him!

As this story illustrates, God can use your business to bring non-Christian co-workers to Himself. But I think God also wants to use you and your business as a witness to your *competitors.* Over the years, I have found that competitors can often be very difficult to love and appreciate. When we first started Sunlight Industries, Al Rosenburg was the marketing director for our largest competitor. His company was doing more business in one month than we did during our entire first year of operation.

I remember envying Al's company, then growing to resent it. His colleagues bad-mouthed our product, tried to undermine our credibility, and lied about us in an effort to take sales away from us.

Every time I drove past his company's offices I found myself becoming angry. But then God began reminding me of Jesus' injunction to "love your enemies." So I began to pray for Al's company and specifically for Al, that God would give me an opportunity to share the Gospel with him.

One day a friend told me that Al's wife had suddenly taken ill and was in the hospital. My wife and I took her some flowers and a book, and the next day Al called to ask if I wanted to go to lunch. I accepted.

During our meal Al said, "Myron, I have watched your company since it started and I want you to know that I greatly admire the way you guys do business."

I was shocked that Al even knew we existed, let alone was aware of our business practices. But then he continued, "You know, there's also something different about you. For example, you came to visit my wife in the hospital. Dave (the head of the company Al worked for) hasn't even bothered to ask how she's doing."

God seemed to whisper in my ear, "Myron, here is your opportunity to tell him about Me." But under my breath I tried to argue with God. "No, this isn't the time," I insisted. I have an appointment as soon as I get back to the office. I don't have enough time!"

But God reminded me of 2 Timothy 4:2, which, as we saw earlier in this chapter, challenges us to share Christ whether it seems convenient or not. So for the next several minutes I told Al about Jesus Christ and about the difference He had made in my life. Then I told him about how I had committed my business to God.

As yet, to my knowledge, Al hasn't become a Christian. But we have become good friends, and I believe God will use my business in Al's life to draw him to Himself.

As we have seen in this chapter, God is interested in people. Once you let God become your senior business partner, He will provide you with ample opportunity to serve the spiritual needs of all kinds of people: employees, competitors, customers, suppliers—even the man on the street.

Your business is the greatest mission field in the world. No one knows your business like you do, and no one has the same type of relationship with your business associates that you do. God has put you where you are because He is concerned about the people you know.

You may be the only real Christian some of these people

have ever known. Don't let them down by getting so involved in the money side of your business that you don't have time for your business' spiritual purpose!

Chapter Summary

In this chapter we examined how Satan has deceived the Christian community into believing that there are two worlds: Our religious world and our secular world. He also has successfully convinced most of us that only a few believers are "called" into full-time Christian service. Finally, he has deceived Christians into thinking that our spiritual lives are private and our secular lives are public, and that we should not offend people in the marketplace by bringing up such private issues as God or religion.

These deceptions have left Satan mostly unopposed as he seeks to control the marketplace and all those who work in it.

The truth, however, is that God has made us a kingdom of priests with the responsibility for relating directly to God and sharing Him with a non-Christian world. Contrary to the notion that God "calls" only a few people into full-time Christian service, He has "called" all of us to preach the Gospel to every person on earth (Mark 16:15). And, as 2 Timothy 4:2 so plainly illustrates, this is a full-time call.

In this chapter we also saw that the Bible clearly states God's purpose and objective for us in the marketplace. We are to reach people with the Gospel. Therefore, if God teams up with us as our senior business partner, we know His goal for our businesses is to be winning people for Christ.

God wants to use you and your business to reach your non-Christian employees, competitors, customers, and any other people with whom you come into contact in the marketplace.

In fact, God truly sees the marketplace as your mission field.

Personal Application

1. Are you ready to begin viewing the marketplace as your mission field? Why or why not?
2. Re-read the chapter. This time through, ask God to begin showing you people (in your company or with whom you do business) for whom you can start praying specifically. Pray that they will come to know Jesus Christ as their Lord and Saviour.
3. Develop an action plan: How can you make yourself available to be used by God in the lives of these people?

6
Biblical Principles
of Business Ethics

When deciding what type of business ethics to follow, Christians have two options. First, we can choose to develop our business ethics as we go—situation by situation. Or, we can opt to define a consistent, constant set of business ethics, and adhere to them—regardless of the situation.

In today's business society, more and more people are choosing option number one. This viewpoint relies on *situation ethics,* and can be defined as *the development of a standard of ethics to fit the needs and requirements of a given situation or transaction.*

The rationale behind situation ethics goes like this: I want to be "fair," but fairness is a relative concept; that is, what one person thinks is fair will not necessarily seem fair to someone else. Therefore, it is impossible to come up with hard and fast *absolute* moral standards when I'm dealing with business ethics. Consequently, I am forced to define my ethics situation by situation—doing what is called for in each instance. That is the only way I can possibly be "fair."

On the surface, the situation ethics approach seems to have a lot going for it. It appears to provide the best possible solution to some very sticky problems. It has one major flaw, however—it is built on humanistic, rather than biblical standards.

As I mentioned earlier, situation ethics disregard the existence of absolutes; therefore, they reject the Bible as being the "final authority" on what is right and wrong. Man makes this determination based on the perceived circumstances of the situation. As a result, right and wrong can potentially change from situation to situation.

I recently saw situation ethics in action. For the past five years, Georgia Rutgers has worked for a printing company in the Northwest. While I was in the area several months ago, she told me that her company had "cheated" her out of a day's vacation time; apparently, there had been a change in policy concerning how vacation time was accumulated.

"But they didn't get away with it," she said angrily. "My husband is an artist. I've taken enough stuff out of the warehouse to keep him in art supplies for a long time."

When I tried to tell her that she was wrong for doing this, she retorted, "Oh, I normally wouldn't steal anything from the company. But, hey, when they steal from me, I have a right to steal from them!"

Georgia Rutgers doesn't claim to be a Christian. Unfortunately, many Christians use the same situation ethics as Georgia.

Remember Don Skinner, the businessman I told you about in the first part of chapter 1? Let's review his story in detail; it's a classic example of how Christians allow themselves to get caught up in the situation ethics mode of doing business.

Referring to his handling of a business deal, Don had said: "Myron, I know some of the people at church might think I'm being unethical, but the stakes were just too high to lose this one." He then explained that he had been "forced" to bribe a purchasing agent in order to land a big contract for his company. According to Don, "I didn't have much choice. My competition was trying to buy them off to get the contract. The client even came to me and said he wanted to do business with my company, but I would have to beat my competition's offer. It was just too good a deal to pass up. So I *beat* their offer."

Don went on to say, "Look, I'm a businessman—not a theologian. You know yourself that it's a dog-eat-dog world out there. Anyway, I look at it this way. As a businessman, I feel my job is to make the money needed to support the church. The more money I make, the more I can give to God's work. And I sure don't see anybody turning it down when the offering plate is passed."

How We Justify Our Use of Situation Ethics

People who employ situation ethics generally do so because they've come to one, or all, of the following conclusions:
- Whatever you try to do to me, I have a right to do to you.
- The "end" justifies the "means."
- Everyone does it, so that makes it OK.
- Go ahead and do it; just don't get caught.
- As long as we all agree, then whatever we do is right.

Don Skinner had adopted a number of these attitudes: He said he "didn't have a choice" regarding his decision to bribe a customer; after all, his competitors already had resorted to this tactic ("Whatever you try to do to me, I have a right to do to you"). He claimed, "It's a dog-eat-dog world out there" ("Everyone does it, so that makes it OK"). He also said, "The more money I make, the more money I can give to God's work" ("The 'end' justifies the 'means' ").

We need to remember, however, that the Bible condemns such "ethical" positions. In contrast to situation ethics' "Whatever you do to me, I have a right to do to you" outlook, Scripture says:

- Do not say, "I'll do to him as he has done to me; I'll pay that man back for what he did" (Prov. 24:29).
- Bless those who persecute you (Rom. 12:14).
- Do not repay anyone evil for evil (Rom. 12:17).
- Do not take revenge (Rom. 12:19).
- If your enemy is hungry, feed him (Rom. 12:20).
- Do not be overcome by evil, but overcome evil with good (Rom. 12:21).

Situation ethics also advise, "Everyone does it, so that makes it OK." But the Apostle Paul says, "Don't copy the behavior and customs of this world" (Rom. 12:2, TLB). And in the Old Testament we are warned, "Do not follow the crowd in doing wrong" (Ex. 23:2). These verses clearly warn us against adopting popular customs and attitudes just because everyone else is following them.

Don Skinner, however, "followed the crowd" in concluding that it was acceptable to bribe his customer; after all, that was what his competition was trying to do. Yet the Bible condemns bribery: "He who gains by oppressing the poor or by bribing the rich shall end in poverty" (Prov. 22:16, TLB). Likewise, in Exodus we are told, "Take no bribes, for a bribe makes you unaware of what you clearly see! A bribe hurts the cause of the person who is right" (23:8, TLB).

We can see, then, that the principles practiced in situation ethics are in direct violation of what God teaches us in the Bible. In fact, they are designed to lead us further and further away from God and His Word.

The Importance of Applying Biblical Business Ethics

We are all familiar with the saying, "Actions speak louder than words." That phrase is particularly important to Christian business people who are operating in a marketplace that's dominated by Satan. We are being watched daily to see if our actions correspond with our words.

If you're a Christian, you are "witnessing" whether you intend to or not. It may not necessarily be an "evangelization witness" per se, but we are "witnessing" just the same. Our peers in the marketplace are watching what we *do* as Christians; not just what we *say*.

It isn't enough, therefore, just to *say* that God is our senior business partner and that He holds the controlling interest in the company. Our actions must demonstrate that this is so. As we discussed in the last chapter, Al Rosenburg, one of our competitors, didn't recognize that our company was "different" by what we *said;* he noticed we were different because of what we *did.*

Since God's "business purpose" is to reach people with the Gospel through us and our businesses, it is imperative that our *business walk* match our *business talk.*

For example, one man I know of owns several businesses. He also is very vocal about his "Christian faith," and is a member of a church board. Because of his questionable business dealings, however, neither Christians nor non-Christians respect him as a businessman—or as a Christian.

One non-Christian business person told me, "If he's an example of what a person learns at church, I'm glad I don't waste my time going." The tragedy is that the person who made that statement adheres more closely to biblical business ethics than the Christian businessman he was discussing.

We must always remember that Jesus set a clear standard for His believers to follow:

> You are the world's seasoning, to make it tolerable.
> If you lose your flavor, what will happen to the world?...You are the world's light—a city on a hill, glowing in the night for all to see. Don't hide your light! Let it shine for all (Matt. 5:13-15, TLB).

Our Lord said that the Christian is to "season" the world so that it is a more tolerable place in which to live. That means Christian business persons are to be the *seasoning* in the marketplace; we are to transform the "dog-eat-dog" environment described by Don Skinner. We must work to replace it with a willingness to treat others in our business deals as we would want to be treated.

In this passage, Jesus also referred to the Christian as "the world's light." In other words, the Christian is to act as a torch; he is to show the frustrated, confused, and fearful masses in the marketplace that they can find help, peace, and workable answers to their problems through Christ.

That is why it is absolutely essential for the Christian business person to practice biblical principles of business ethics. The world is looking on, wondering if we really *do* have the answers—if Christianity actually *does* work. Can one really know God personally? Will He help me on a day-to-day basis?

Later in Matthew we are told *why* we are to be the seasoning and light in the marketplace: "So that they will praise your Heavenly Father" (5:16, TLB). Notice that we don't practice biblical business ethics to indicate our superiority over other people. We do so in order to attract people in the marketplace to God.

How Do I Know What Is Biblically Ethical?

Once a person is committed to applying biblical principles of business ethics, he still must determine what is, and is not, ethical. Most Christian business people I know who are committed to obeying God's Word share a similar trait. They would like to be able to open their Bibles and find an immediate answer to every business ethics problem that confronts them. But that is not possible.

Even though the Bible *does* deal specifically with many business ethics issues, it usually emphasizes *principles* rather than specific facts or "how to's."

For example, the Lord has commanded us to "Remember the Sabbath Day by keeping it holy" (Ex. 20:8).

That sounds like a simple enough statement. But what exactly does it mean to "keep the Sabbath holy?" And how do I know when I'm being obedient to that biblical requirement? If you think the answers to these questions are that straightforward, call ten different pastors from ten different denominations in your city. Ask them to define specifically what you must do to keep the Sabbath holy. I guarantee you that before you are halfway through your list, you'll be pulling your hair out in confusion and frustration.

Some—but not all—of these pastors will tell you that to

keep the Sabbath holy, you shouldn't work on Sunday. Well, that also seems simple enough. But what is work? Some will tell you that it includes such activities as mowing the lawn, painting your house, or cleaning the garage. Therefore, to keep the Sabbath holy, you simply should worship God and rest the remainder of the day.

Others, however, might say that if you find mowing the lawn and painting the house relaxing (because they're a break in your regular "work routine"), then it's OK to engage in those activities.

By now you're really confused. You found a simple biblical instruction, and when you started to apply it, you thought you'd have no problems. But when you asked a group of Bible experts to interpret this instruction, you got so many different opinions that you didn't know what to do.

The Bible often is very specific. For example, the injunction, "You shall not steal" (Ex 20:15), is quite unambiguous. On the other hand, when God tells us through His Word that we should "remember the Sabbath Day by keeping it holy," we aren't told exactly *how* to fulfill this commandment.

Because of this particular dilemma, Jewish religious leaders came up with elaborate lists of do's and don'ts to explain exactly what they *thought* God meant when He gave particular commandments (such as keeping the Sabbath holy). As a result, the people went to these religious leaders to find out what God wanted them to do—rather than going directly to God Himself.

Consequently, ancient Israel went from having a relationship with God to guarding a formula of shoulds and should nots that was passed from one person to another. God was left out of the picture. Finally the laws of man became more well known and important than the laws of God.

That caused Jesus to tell the religious leaders of His day, "You have let go of the commands of God and are holding on to the traditions of men. . . . You have a fine way of setting aside the commands of God in order to observe your own traditions!" (Mark 7:8-9)

The fact is, God stresses *principles* over *lists* because He wants us to bring these principles to Him; He wants us to interact with Him and discuss exactly how they ought to be lived out in our lives. That is how we develop and maintain a "personal relationship" with God. We don't develop a relationship with Him simply by reading a list of do's and don'ts and methodically following it.

Therefore, when it comes to developing biblical principles of business ethics, we must take certain principles to God, discuss them with Him, and do what *He* tells us to do. Then, instead of making a list of do's and don'ts out of this instruction, and teaching it to other business people as *absolute biblical law*, we should simply tell our colleagues, "This is what God told me to do. But you should discuss the principle with Him for yourself, and then do whatever He tells you." If your friends come back and say, "When I talked to God, He told me to do it another way," we must be careful not to judge them. We can't say, "I knew you weren't as spiritual as I am. You're doing it all wrong; you must do it *my* way!"

The Key Biblical Statements Concerning Business Ethics

From time to time people have approached me and said, "Myron, you should write a book on what the Bible teaches on business ethics. There's sure a need for one." As I discussed this request further with them, I discovered that in most cases, these people really were looking for their own copy of the old pharisaical law. They, like the people of the Old Testament, were asking for a list of religious do's and don'ts to help run their businesses. I'd *never* want to write *that* type of book!

In this chapter, however, I do want to pass on what I consider to be the foundational passage in the Bible concerning business ethics. I feel this verse is the foundation because it provides a very precise and consistent principle; yet at the same time, it requires us to go to God—situation by situation—to find out how He wants us to apply the principle.

Having stated this, it is now time to unveil our foundational verse:

> In everything, do to others what you would have them do to you, for this sums up the Law and the Prophets (Matt. 7:12).

This is the verse on which all biblical principles of business ethics rest. It is the key principle for running your business according to biblical standards. It is the way God, your senior business partner, does business! If you consistently apply this one biblical principle, your business dealings with people in the marketplace will always be in accordance with what God wants.

Let's look at the verse point by point. It starts off by saying "In *everything*." This is an all-inclusive phrase. It encompasses *every* business situation and transaction. It covers dealings with our employees, competition, customers, friends, enemies, and the total stranger we meet in the marketplace. *It means that at all times, in all places, with all people, we are consistently to apply this principle!*

Now let's look at the principle expressed in the words, "Do to others what you would have them do to you." What a simple but profound principle. Its application insures proper business ethics at all times. It implies that we should simply treat others the way we would want them to treat us.

Notice, however, that this principle does *not* say "treat others the way *they* want to be treated." But what's wrong with that? Consider the following story.

While I was negotiating a contract with a federal agency recently, the contracting officer tried to persuade me to perform some additional services without offering me additional payment. He knew I was a Christian, so he said, "Come on, Myron. Remember, you're to do unto others as you would have them do unto you."

Obviously, this man thought that Jesus' instruction meant, "If you are a Christian, you're supposed to do what other people want you to do." But that is *not* what the verse teaches. The principle is: *In a given situation, treat people just as you would want them to treat you in that situation.*

For example, if you are paying an employee $5 an hour to do a certain type of job—but you know that if you were the employee performing the same task, you'd think the job was worth $6 an hour—then you are violating biblical principles of business ethics. You aren't treating the employee as you'd want to be treated in that same situation. You are, in fact, cheating the employee out of $1 per hour. And according to Matthew 7:12, you are being unethical.

Remember this verse says, "Do to others what *you* would have *them* do to you." Of course, that doesn't mean that your employees always have to agree with your business decisions concerning them; it *does* mean, though, that if you were in *their* situations, you'd be content and convinced that you were being treated fairly.

Let's look again at the entire verse: "In everything, do to others what you would have them do to you, for this sums up the Law and the Prophets." Did you catch that last phrase, "for this *sums up* the Law and the Prophets"? This verse summarizes all the teachings of God-given Old Testament Law as well as the principles and teachings of the Prophets.

That is why this verse is the *foundation* for all biblical principles of business ethics. If we apply it conscientiously, we are doing everything that God teaches in His Law.

There also is another important passage for us to consider when we are trying to develop and implement biblical principles of business ethics. It too is found in Matthew:

If you are slapped on one cheek, turn the other too. If you are ordered to court, and your shirt is taken from you, give your coat too. If the military demand that you carry their gear for a mile, carry it two. Give to those who ask, and don't turn away from those who want to borrow (5:39-42, TLB).

This is a very difficult passage for most business people to accept and understand. It seems to go against every fiber of our business nature. Actually, it goes against every fiber of our *human, carnal* nature.

Jesus is teaching us a great truth in this passage. And like the message we saw earlier in Matthew 7:12, it plays a key role in the development of biblical business ethics.

Simply stated, the principle Jesus is teaching us in this passage is this: *Always be committed to giving beyond what people and the law require you to give.*

This principle represents the very essence of our Lord's teachings in the New Testament. God doesn't want us to do *only* what people and the law expect and require of us. Even most *non*-Christians in the marketplace do that (Matt. 5:46-47). Rather, He wants us to be committed to serving people and going that extra mile for them.

Everyone expects us to do what is required. But it's when we do *more* than is anticipated that people realize we are different from other business persons in the marketplace. And when people see that we are different, at some point, they are going to want to know *why*. We'll then have an opportunity to tell them that we are running our businesses on biblical principles.

Developing a Statement of Ethics

Every business should have a statement of ethics that serves as the "rudder" to guide all of its business dealings and transactions. Personally, I feel that such a statement should incorporate the principles taught in the two biblical passages we've examined in this chapter.

Your statement of ethics will become your statement to the marketplace, telling others how they can expect to be treated when they do business with you.

My own personal statement of ethics is as follows:

With God's help, in each situation, I will always endeavor to treat you the way I would want and expect you to treat me in the same situation. And, with God's assistance, I will always be committed to giving beyond what people and the law require of me in whatever act of service my business and I are involved in.

There are several ways I could have approached this chapter. I could have developed a list of situations that commonly confront businessmen, and then discussed how *I* thought various scriptural passages provided ethical guidelines for those situations.

But, my list might not have corresponded with your needs; and you may not have agreed with *my* interpretation of the meaning of the passages as they relate to business ethics. On the other hand, if you had *agreed* with my interpretation, you might have been tempted simply to accept my views without personally discussing your questions with God.

That's why I thought it best to present some of the passages that provide us with key principles for developing a biblical approach to business ethics. I challenge you to take those passages and principles and list some of the ethical dilemmas associated with running your business. Then talk to God, your senior business partner, and ask for His input in applying the biblical principles presented in this chapter.

As you do this, I believe four things will happen:

(1) Your relationship with God will improve.

(2) You will develop proper business ethics based solely on God's Word.

(3) People in the marketplace—as well as in your own company—will recognize that your Christian talk and your Christian walk are the same.

(4) You and God will be much more effective in accomplishing your joint goals for the business.

Chapter Summary

Christians are faced with two options when dealing with business ethics. We can either follow the philosophy of the world, or we can follow the teachings of God in the Bible. We can't do both.

The world has adopted a philosophy called situation ethics, which says, in effect, that there are no moral absolutes. People who adhere to situation ethics usually embrace the following beliefs:

(1) Whatever you try to do to me, I have a right to do to you.
(2) The "end" justifies the "means."
(3) Everyone does it this way, so that makes it OK.
(4) Go ahead and do it; just don't get caught.
(5) As long as we all agree, then whatever we do is right.

Yet Christ tells us, "In everything, do to others what you would have them do to you, for this sums up the Law and the Prophets" (Matt. 7:12). This is the foundation passage on which all biblical principles of business ethics are developed.

Notice that the verse applies to all people, in all situations, at all times. It says, "in everything"—which is all-inclusive.

Matthew 5:39-42 gives us another important principle. In it the Lord states that we should always be committed to giving beyond what people and the law require us to give.

Most people do what is required of them, but few people do more. Yet it is precisely by exceeding such expectations that the marketplace recognizes Christians as being different. As people realize that we do not operate like the rest of the world, they will be more open to hearing about God. And that is one of the major reasons God has placed us in the marketplace.

Personal Application

1. Study Matthew 7:12 and memorize it.
   a. What are the things that tend to hinder you from applying that verse in your life and business?

    b. Why does Satan try to get us to use the world's approach instead of God's?

    c. Make a list of ethical issues in your business and determine how you will apply this verse in establishing your business ethics.

2. Read Matthew 5:39-42 and meditate on it.

    a. How should you be applying the principle, "Always be committed to giving beyond what people and the law require you to give"?

    b. How do you think the application of that principle will affect your business?

3. Develop a statement of ethics for your company. Begin communicating that statement to both your employees and customers.

7
The Seven Laws
of Business Success

The Madison Avenue Success Syndrome has our society firmly in its grasp. Local bookstores carry a wide variety of "how-to" books that promise you success in everything from your sex life to your tennis game. They tell you how to climb the corporate ladder, how to dress on the way up, and how to cope with success once you get it.

In this chapter we will compare the world's view of success with God's. We will look at what it means to have a "Christian" business, and examine the "laws" that develop and govern true business success.

How the World Defines Success
Once a person becomes a Christian, it doesn't take long for him or her to recognize that there is a big difference between the thoughts and actions of the world, and what the Bible teaches.

Several times in this book I've mentioned that Satan is a master at deception. For every true principle that God teaches, Satan has a counterfeit. And that certainly holds true when it comes to defining success.

I recently saw a newspaper ad promoting a local seminar. The headline of the ad read, "Come and Learn the Secrets of Success." I decided to go; I wanted to get in on these "secrets."

The room was packed with people ranging in age from their early 20s to late 60s. The speaker opened his seminar by stating: "I am here today to show you how you can make as much money as you want. You soon will be able to achieve whatever level of success you are after in life."

Like this individual, some people think success is measured by their ability to *buy things*. They believe the more "things" you have, or are capable of buying, the more successful you are. They tend to judge your success by the size of your purchases—how big a house you live in, how many cars you have, how many trips you've taken, etc. To these people, money is the basis for success; the more money you have, the more things you can buy.

Other people measure success in terms of *achievements* rather than money. The more you're able to accomplish, the more successful you are. In fact, a very popular definition of success states: "Success is the progressive achievement of a worthwhile goal."

People strive for success because in it they imagine they will find happiness, peace, joy, and fulfillment. However, when they follow the world's approach to success, none of their happiness, peace, joy, or fulfillment is lasting. Sometimes they discover—too late—that they have been deceived in their understanding of what constitutes success.

During his lifetime, J. Paul Getty was one of the richest men in the world. From the profits of his oil company, he had purchased all the "things" money could buy. His achievements were almost limitless. However, as he neared the end of his life, he said, "All my wealth and success was not able to produce a happy marriage." Getty had discovered that all the achievements in the world could not produce lasting happiness, peace, joy, or fulfillment.

The words of an old song remind us, "Everything that glitters is not gold." That certainly applies to the world's view of success and how to achieve it. Far too many people in the marketplace have given their entire lives to the pursuit of things, money, and achievements. Yet they've often discovered that, in the final analysis, following the world's definitions of success left them empty and unfulfilled.

How the Bible Defines Success

God says:

> For My thoughts are not your thoughts, neither are your ways My ways.... As the heavens are higher than the earth, so are My ways higher than your ways and My thoughts than your thoughts (Isa. 55:8-9).

This passage clearly points out that God's values, principles, and actions usually are diametrically opposed to the world's.

This does not mean that it is wrong to have "things." We saw in chapter 3 that God promises to supply material possessions when we seek His kingdom first. And it doesn't mean that it is wrong to pursue goals and value our achievements. However, when our measures for success become "things

and achievements," we are settling for far less than the true
success God has available for us.

Notice what Paul says to the Philippians:

> But all these things that I once thought very worth-
> while—now I've thrown them all away so that I can
> put my trust and hope in Christ alone. Yes, every-
> thing else is worthless when compared with the
> priceless gain of knowing Christ (3:7-8, TLB).

It is important that we understand something about Paul,
the man who made that statement. He had studied under
Gamaliel and was highly educated. He was a Pharisee, a
member of the elite religious and political group of the Jews.
He also was a Roman citizen—a great honor of his day. And
he was a businessman—a skilled tentmaker.

Yet Paul came to realize that true success wasn't found in
the things he had acquired or the achievements he had
made. He said all those things were "worthless when compared with the priceless gain of having Christ." In essence,
then, the apostle is saying that we are truly successful when
we make Jesus Christ Lord of our lives.

But why is that? Notice Jesus' words recorded in John's
Gospel: "The thief's purpose is to steal, kill, and destroy. My
purpose is to give life in all its fullness" (10:10, TLB). In other
words, not only does Jesus Christ give us eternal life and a
home in heaven, He also gives us life *"in all its fullness."*
Now that's *true* success. And it comes by accepting Christ as
our personal Lord and Saviour and then by letting Him direct
His plans and purpose through us and our businesses.

The world is desperately searching for "life in all its fullness." But it is looking in all the wrong places. Satan has
deceived people in the marketplace into looking for the full

life we call success in "things" and achievements, instead of in Jesus Christ.

Such people need to be introduced to the truths we've just considered. Paul teaches us from personal experience that to know Jesus Christ is the key to *real* success. In fact, he said everything else is "worthless when compared with the priceless gain of having Christ."

For the remainder of the chapter, then, we will look at how a knowledge of Christ provides the foundation for principles or "laws" that can help you experience success in your life and business.

Law One: Always Put God First in Your Life and Business

We are told in Deuteronomy to "love the Lord your God with all your heart and with all your soul and with all your strength" (6:5). In short, this verse instructs us to put God first with our total being—heart, soul, and strength.

There are two important reasons for putting God first in our lives and businesses. First, God will not settle for *second* place. He will be Lord of all—or not at all. Remember the statement we saw earlier in Matthew:

No one can serve two masters. Either he will hate the one and love the other, or he will be devoted to the one and despise the other. You cannot serve both God and Money (6:24).

The first of the Ten Commandments recorded in Exodus lets us know exactly how God feels about being first in our lives. He says, "You shall have no other gods before Me" (20:3). In other words, nothing in our lives is to come ahead of God—not our businesses, not making money, not our families. *Nothing!*

The second reason for putting God first in your life and business is found in Matthew: "But seek first His kingdom and His righteousness, and all these things will be given to you as well" (6:33).

This verse indicates that when God is first in your life and business, all the things the pagans seek first in *their* lives (money, things, achievements) will be *given* to you by Him—according to what is best for you.

If God is not first in your life and business, then *you* have to rely on *your own* resourcefulness to succeed in business. If God is first in your business, however, He becomes the resource for producing success. Imagine that! When God is first in your life and business, you have His unlimited power and resources behind you . You can't find a better backer for your business than that!

The Bible clearly testifies to God's power: "I know that You can do all things; no plan of Yours can be thwarted" (Job 42:2). And, "Nothing is impossible with God" (Luke 1:37).

I don't know about you, but I feel very secure placing God first in my business. I will take His resources over my resourcefulness any day! Putting God first in your business is truly the first and most important step to experiencing life "in all its fullness."

Law Two: Get to Know God's Word and Apply It to Your Life and Business

Unfortunately, it seems that many Christian business people know very little of God's Word—the Bible—and even less about how it applies to their day-to-day transactions in the marketplace.

The Bible is the best textbook on business that has ever

been written. It gives us principles on everything from business finance to decision-making to how to evaluate employee performance. The Bible is truly the best authority available on how to develop and operate a successful business.

Accordingly, it is important that you "Do not let this Book of the Law depart from your mouth, meditate on it day and night, so that you may be careful to do everything written in it. Then you will be prosperous and successful" (Josh. 1:8).

This verse tells us that we should be spending time *daily* studying and meditating on God's Word. Next, it encourages us to *apply* everything we learn from it. And as we do, it promises that we will be prosperous and successful.

This isn't the only verse that makes such a claim. Notice what the Psalms tell us:

God's laws are perfect. They protect us, make us wise, and give us joy and light. God's laws are pure, eternal, just. They are more desirable than gold. They are sweeter than honey dripping from a honeycomb. For they warn us away from harm and give success to those who obey them (Ps. 19:7-11, TLB).

What a fantastic description of God's Word and its value and benefits to those who obey it! This passage says that God's laws and principles are *perfect, eternal, pure,* and *just.* That is very comforting.

I don't know of any other book dealing with business principles which can claim that all of its principles are "perfect." And certainly no other book can claim that its principles are eternal. Today, theories on business change like the weather. It's also important to note that each of the business principles presented in the Bible is just and fair to all concerned—the owner, employees, customers, and competition. This passage points out too that God's Word is "more desirable than gold." That's because the Bible tells us how to earn gold, what to do with it when we get it, and finally, how to be truly happy whether or not we have it.

Lastly, this passage mentions that God's Word "warns us away from harm and gives success to those who obey" it. Scripture protects us from making wrong decisions and gives us the principles of business success. But, it ends with a condition for receiving all these wonderful benefits: *We first have to obey what it says!*

Russ Johnston, a close friend and businessman from Colorado Springs, began a project a few years ago converting an apartment complex into condominiums. Recently Russ told me, "When we started the project, we decided to apply God's principles of doing business to every situation and transaction." He went on to say, "As we prayed about it, we decided we should close our sales office on Sunday. We felt God was telling us to do that to keep the Sabbath holy."

He pointed out that their sales office was the only one in the area that closed on Sunday. At times they felt a lot of pressure to open on Sunday, as that was when most people went out to look at homes. "But I know from firsthand experience that it pays to apply God's principles of doing business," he concluded. "Of all the condo conversion projects going on in this town, ours was the only one to be totally completed in the past five years—even though most of the other companies spent a lot more time, energy, and money promoting their projects than we did."

Like Russ Johnston, you too can experience success—even when others may fail—as you learn to apply God's Word daily in your business. You can't use it, however, if you don't *know* it! So get acquainted with Scripture and apply it consistently in your life and business.

Law Three: Expect Big Things from a Big God

Once we put God first in our lives and businesses, and begin studying and applying His Word on a daily basis, we can anticipate receiving wonderful things from a wonderful God.

What are the goals for your business this year? Next year? Five years from now? Are you aware that God has unlimited power and resources available to you to accomplish great things with your life and business?

Paul confirms the truth of this fact in his Epistle to the Ephesians:

> Now glory be to God who by His mighty power at work within us is able to do far more than we would ever dare to ask or even dream of—infinitely beyond our highest prayers, desires, thoughts, or hopes (3:20, TLB).

What a fantastic promise! God says that He has power available to work in us to accomplish *more* than we could ever ask for or dream of.

The God who wants to be your senior business partner is a big God. It was your senior business partner who said:

> "Let there be light," and there was light.... "Let the land produce vegetation"... and it was so.... "Let the water teem with living creatures"... and God saw that it was good.... "Let us make man in Our image."... So God created man in His own image (Gen. 1:3, 11, 20-21, 26-27).

Can you name a non-Christian business person anywhere

who has a partner capable of producing anything *close* to that? Our God has *unlimited power,* and that power is available to *all* believers.

Like the Children of Israel, however, many of us are reluctant to take God up on His offer. In the Book of Joshua, we are told that even after God gave the Israelites the Promised Land, and they had been there a considerable amount of time, over half the tribes still had failed to take possession of the land. That led Joshua to ask them: "How long will you wait before you begin to take possession of the land that the Lord, the God of your fathers, has given you?" (Josh. 18:3)

The fact is, God had given His children the land, but they were reluctant to accept His gift. You may say, "If God had given *me* that land, I sure wouldn't hesitate to take it!" But God has offered us something far more valuable. He has made His unlimited power available to us; yet most of us ignore His offer and attempt to use our meager energies to compete successfully for business in the marketplace.

Earlier, I asked what your goals were. A person usually does not set goals that he or she knows cannot be accomplished. Therefore, if we are relying on our human energies to accomplish our goals, we'll limit them to ones we think we can achieve; our aims won't be nearly as big as the ones we'd set if we were trusting God and His unlimited power.

Your business will never reach its full potential for success until you begin setting goals that rely on God's ability to achieve them. Go ahead. Expect big things from a big God!

Law Four: Place More Value in People Than in Products
I recently received a letter from a manufacturing company. The firm's slogan was printed across the top of the letterhead;

it read, "Our product is our most prized possession."

When I saw that, I felt sorry both for the company's employees and for the customers who use its services. If you want to be truly successful in business, *people* must be all important. And that doesn't just mean the customers who purchase your product or services. That means everyone who's involved with your business.

To be genuinely successful, we must align our priorities with those of God, our senior business partner. And God makes it very clear that people are His top priority. The product which our company produces is only the tool through which we serve people. We use the product to supply jobs for our employees. We use the product to serve a need of our customers. And we use the product to generate a cash flow so that the needs of our employees and customers can continue to be met.

That doesn't mean we should neglect the quality of our product or service. In Colossians we read, "Whatever you do, work at it with all your heart, as working for the Lord, not for men" (3:23). This verse makes it clear that we are to provide the best product possible.

The point I'm trying to make, though, is that to be successful in business from God's perspective, we must put people first. They are all-important.

This concept is further illustrated in Matthew's Gospel. Here, Christ says, products do not take precedence over people. "What good will it be for a man if he gains the whole world, yet forfeits his soul? Or what can a man give in exchange for his soul?" (16:26) This verse alludes to the immeasurable value of the individual. God is claiming that one person is more valuable than all the wealth in the world.

That's why God's major objective for your business is people. He wants you to see the same value in people that He does. It is only as this occurs that God is free to use your business to reach people in the marketplace and stifle Satan's plans to control commerce.

We must keep in mind that the angels in heaven rejoice more over one person who accepts Jesus Christ than they do over all the profits we make in a lifetime! Therefore, don't lose sight of your business priorities; and remember, people are far more valuable than any product produced in the marketplace.

Law Five: Give God the Pick of Your Profits

If God is your senior business partner, then He should be allowed to decide how your company's profits will be spent. Scripture unabashedly supports this concept.

> Honor the Lord by giving Him the first part of all your income, and He will fill your barns with wheat and barley and overflow your wine vats with the finest wines (Prov. 3:9-10, TLB).

You'll notice that there is a promise attached to this command: If you give God the first portion of *all* your income (that means income from any source), then in return, He will bless you materially. This promise is reinforced in Proverbs:

> One man gives freely, yet gains even more; another withholds unduly, but comes to poverty. A generous man will prosper; he who refreshes others will himself be refreshed (11:24-25).

So how does God want you to spend your money? Well, in addition to giving to your local church and favorite missions organizations, He commands you to give to the poor. Notice what Proverbs again tells us: "When you help the poor you are lending to the Lord—and He pays wonderful interest on your loan!" (19:17, TLB)

What a great verse! It lets us know that we have an obligation to help the poor and needy. As we respond to this obligation, we're making a sound investment—because God pays great interest on the money we invest in the poor.

In fact, such giving lays up treasures in heaven.

Tell those who are rich not to be proud and not to trust in their money, which will soon be gone, but their pride and trust should be in the living God who always richly gives us all we need for our enjoyment. Tell them to use their money to do good. They should be rich in good works and should give happily to those in need, always being ready to share with others whatever God has given them. By doing this they will be storing up real treasure for themselves in heaven—it is the only safe investment for eternity! And they will be living a fruitful Christian life down here as well (1 Tim. 6:17-19, TLB).

Your best investment as a business person, then, is to share what you have with those in need. When you do, God not only will give you a great present return on your investment, but He'll be crediting treasures to your "heavenly account." Where else can you find a deal like that?

Law Six: Be Committed to Honesty and Integrity

The author of Proverbs tells us that "The Lord demands fairness in every business deal. He established this principle" (16:11, TLB).

The essence of this verse is that God *demands* fairness at all times in business. It is not an option for the Christian business person. God insists on it! Notice too that the verse tells us that it was God who established the principle of honesty and integrity in business.

This same principle also is expressed in Deuteronomy: "You must have accurate and honest weights and measures, so that you may live long in the land the Lord your God is giving you" (25:15). God again is indicating that the practice of honesty and integrity carries tremendous benefits. The Lord is equally clear, however, in outlining the shortcomings of dishonesty in business dealings: "Dishonest gain will never last, so why take the risk? Because the wicked are unfair, their violence boomerangs and destroys them" (Prov. 21:6-7, TLB).

In short, this verse is pointing out that it is risky business to practice dishonesty. Profits derived in such a manner will not last.

However, some people in business have been deceived into thinking that dishonesty and cheating are nothing more than *shrewd business practices*. If an entrepreneur can squeeze more money out of a deal through slightly shady practices, who's to care? But the Bible firmly opposes that idea. It claims that people who cheat in business will wind up losing both their money *and* their businesses.

So, if you want your business to be truly successful and lasting, make sure you're committed to honest and fair business practices!

Law Seven: Be Diligent in Your Pursuit of Business Success
According to Scripture, "Lazy hands make a man poor, but diligent hands bring wealth" (Prov. 10:4) and, "The sluggard

craves and gets nothing, but the desires of the diligent are fully satisfied" (Prov. 13:4). These verses are significant in that they instruct the Christian business person to be diligent. He must be diligent in pursuing the laws of business success presented in this chapter, and in terms of his work habits. These two verses from Proverbs thus suggest that diligence is one of the important keys to wealth and success.

I want to challenge you to implement these seven laws of business success. Make them a part of your personal and business life. Then watch God begin to accomplish things with you and your business that you never dreamed possible.

Chapter Summary

According to the world, success is measured by your ability to buy things and achieve results. The more "things" you possess—houses, cars, and so on—and the greater your accomplishments, the more successful the world says you are. Yet in Ecclesiastes we read that things and achievements are meaningless: they are akin to "chasing after the wind" (2:11).

Expanding on this concept in his letter to the Philippians, Paul states, "But all these things that I once thought very worthwhile—now I've thrown them all away so that I can put my trust and hope in Christ alone. Yes, everything else is worthless when compared with the priceless gain of knowing Christ" (3:7-8, TLB).

Paul is saying here that things and accomplishments are not nearly as worthwhile as knowing Jesus Christ as one's personal Lord and Saviour. Having that type of relationship with Him is the basis for *true* success.

Once we've placed Christ in charge of our lives, we can then understand biblical principles of business success—of

which there are seven:
(1) Always put God first in your life and business.
(2) Get to know God's Word and apply it to your life and business.
(3) Expect big things from a big God.
(4) Place more value in people than in products.
(5) Give God the pick of your profits.
(6) Be committed to honesty and integrity.
(7) Be diligent in your pursuit of business success.

Personal Application
Study the seven laws of business success—one at a time—and develop a plan of action for making them a part of your life and business.

8
How God Turns Our Failures into Success

Failures are the stepping-stones to success. One Midwestern man's life thoroughly exemplified this principle. In 1832 this gentleman's problems began when he lost his job. In that same year he ran for the state legislature but was defeated. In 1834, he failed in yet another business. And if that weren't bad enough, his sweetheart died the following year. In 1836 he suffered a nervous breakdown.

By that time, he had gone through enough failures to last most people a lifetime. But his were just beginning.

In 1834, he lost a congressional election, though he finally did win a seat in the U.S. House of Representatives in 1846. His success, however, was short-lived; he was defeated for reelection in 1848. The next year he tried to secure a job as a land officer but was rejected. Then in 1854 he ran for the U.S. Senate—and lost. Two years later, his name was suggested as a potential vice-presidential candidate; another man was chosen instead. In 1858, he again ran for the Senate. Again, he lost.

However, in 1860, he actually was elected President of the United States. His name? Abraham Lincoln! As much as any man in American history, Lincoln proved that failures are valuable training courses for future success.

Abraham Lincoln lost one job and was turned down for another, suffered the death of his sweetheart, went through a nervous breakdown and was defeated for political office several times before he finally became President of the United States. He truly learned to use his failures as stepping-stones to success.

Yet it isn't Lincoln's failures for which he is remembered. Rather, we recall his successes as a great statesman. In fact, I suspect that many people aren't even aware of Lincoln's many failures. But all of us know of his success. Thus, it isn't the setbacks in life which should concern us; it's how we *handle* them that's important. The fact is, our abilities to manage our *current* failures will determine our abilities to succeed in the *future.*

God Sees Our Failures as Opportunities

For the Christian, failure is largely a matter of perspective. We sometimes see a particular failure as being a harbinger of disaster. In some instances, our situations might be so bad that we want to give up on life, tuck our tails between our legs, and hide from the rest of the world.

But, did you know that God always looks on the Christian's failures as great *opportunities?* For in our despair, God can show us—and the rest of the world—His mighty power as He rescues us.

"I want you to trust Me in your times of trouble," the Lord says, "so I can rescue you, and you can give Me glory" (Ps. 50:15, TLB). First of all, God is telling us through this verse that there *will* be "times of trouble." Just because we are Christian business people doesn't mean we will escape all of the troubles, problems, and disasters that "secular" businesses go through.

I frequently talk to Christian businessmen who think that because they're Christians, they somehow are immune to the problems and setbacks that non-Christian entrepreneurs experience. That just isn't true.

Not only does the psalmist tell us that we will live through times of trouble, but Jeremiah alludes to the *intensity* of these troubles:

But blessed is the man who trusts in the Lord, whose confidence is in Him. He will be like a tree planted by the water that sends out its roots by the stream. It does not fear when heat comes; its leaves are always green. It has no worries in a year of drought and never fails to bear fruit (Jer. 17:7-8).

This passage points out that the godly will have troubles and failures. Even though Jeremiah refers to people "whose confidence is in Him," he goes on to say that the heat will come and that an occasional year of drought will arrive. But even in the toughest of times, God rescues those who trust in Him: "I want you to trust Me in your times of trouble, so I can rescue you" (Ps. 50:15, TLB).

Just think of it: *While I am in the process of failing, God is in the process of lining up His resources and power to rescue me!* While I am thinking that an opportunity is lost, God is rejoicing at the opportunity to help me.

And why is God so eager to help us when we have trouble or fail? "I want you to trust Me in your times of trouble, so I can rescue you, and *you can give Me glory*" (Ps. 50:15; italics mine). God wants to rescue us when we fail because that is how we—and the rest of the world—can learn He is a personal God; He is the One who is willing and has the power to help us through any problem we may encounter.

If we solve our own problems, who gets the credit? *We do*—and other business people either envy or admire us for our business savvy. But if we trust God when we have a problem, and He rescues us from the situation, who gets the credit? God does!

Therefore, God wants to turn your failures into successes so that we—and business people in the marketplace—will learn that He is concerned about the business person's problems. The Lord will solve them if only we trust Him and let Him be our business partner.

The Value of Failures
Most people view failure as a negative experience. The Bible says, however, that we should look at our failures as positive learning experiences that can help develop our characters and enlarge our personal capabilities.

James clearly describes the value which problems and failures can assume in our lives:

> Dear brothers, is your life full of difficulties and temptations? Then be happy, for when the way is rough, your patience has a chance to grow. So let it grow, and don't try to squirm out of your problems. For when your patience is finally in full bloom, then you will be ready for anything, strong in character,

full and complete" (1:2-4, TLB).

In this passage, God is teaching us that failures can have great value in our lives. In fact, it is out of our failures and difficulties that we learn the principles that produce success.

In order to appreciate the full benefit of this passage, let's dissect it, point by point.

First, it explains that we should be happy when failures, problems, and difficulties come our way. ("Dear brothers, is your life full of difficulties and temptations? Then be happy.") But isn't this response just the opposite of our normal reactions to problems?

Our attitudes usually are the first things to be affected by problems and failures. We are tempted to say, "Why me?" We tend to start focusing on all the negative aspects of a situation.

One day, for example, I got a call from Raymond Sutton, owner of a Canadian trucking company. He phoned to discuss the problems he was having with his business.

Raymond had a long-term contract with a mining company to haul ore from the company's mines to a mill. When the mines began to increase production after acquiring new Japanese contracts, Raymond bought three new, expensive ore-hauling trucks in anticipation of an increased workload. But, a few months after he made this purchase, the mining company notified Raymond that it actually was *cutting back* on production because of a prolonged labor strike at the Japanese firm. As a result, Ray found himself with three trucks too many, and was unable to make the payments on the loan he had taken out to buy them. The bank had just called to tell him he had two weeks to come up with several thousand dollars in back payments. If he failed to do so, the bank would take the trucks, plus some land he had used for collateral on the down payment.

When Raymond called he was mad at God, the Japanese, the mining company, the bank, and his wife—for telling him he should be praying to God instead of being mad at Him. I almost made Raymond mad at *me* when I told him I agreed with his wife.

"Why should I pray to God?" he half yelled over the phone. "I prayed a year ago for His help in getting a good deal on the trucks, and I got a super deal. But if God knew this was going to happen, why did He let me buy those trucks? I'm about to lose them *and* a piece of ground that I intended to build a summer cabin on. Some friend God turned out to be!"

I never was able to get Raymond to accept the fact that God could, and would, use the situation for a positive result—*if he would just trust Him.*

Regrettably, Raymond is a classic example of how Satan uses our problems and failures to make us blame God, ourselves, and others for a bad situation. Satan knows that if he can get us to focus on "negatives" rather than on positive lessons from a situation, he has won a major victory in our lives. He also has cheated us out of the opportunity to learn how to be mature enough to develop and handle real success in the future.

However, as alluded to above, to learn from our failures, we first must be willing to focus on "positives." We need to realize that God has allowed the situation to come into our lives and, as Psalm 50:15 points out, He will rescue us so we can give Him the glory. What's more, God can use our failures to transform us into more capable, mature people—people who are able to achieve success and handle it once we have it.

That is why the passage in James which we considered earlier starts by telling us to be happy when we have problems and trials.

This passage also teaches us we should not try to squirm out of our problems. We should accept responsibility for the failure, and unlike Raymond Sutton, not attempt to blame others for our own decisions.

The only way a failure can be of value to us is if we are willing to accept our part in causing it. As long as we try to place all the fault and blame on others, we'll never admit or recognize that our own weaknesses and faults contributed to the problem. When dealing with failures it is far more productive to focus on *solutions,* rather than spending time trying to place the blame on others for the problem. By maintaining a positive attitude and accepting responsibility for the problem we will: (1) "be ready for anything," (2) become "strong in character," and (3) become "full and complete" people.

The "Overcomer" Attitude

The "sweet smell of success" always comes from the flowers that are watered by the tears of our failures. The only difference between successful business people and unsuccessful ones is that the successful individuals overcame their failures; the unsuccessful ones didn't.

As we saw in James 1:2-4, one of the results of overcoming failure is that it gives us "ready for anything" dispositions. I call this the "overcomer attitude."

The way to develop an "overcomer attitude" is to face your failure head on, admit you blew it, accept responsibility for it, trust God to rescue you from it, and learn how to avoid it. When you do this, as James points out (1:4), you'll find yourself ready to face any challenge. Once you've witnessed God's "rescuing power," you'll be able to tackle big problems in the future, knowing that God is capable of handling anything you can't.

Abraham Lincoln became President because he was an overcomer. Had he not learned to be an overcomer, he would never have made it past his first political defeat. But his "overcomer attitude" carried him over numerous political failures on his road to the White House.

The Apostle Paul also was an overcomer. In 2 Corinthians he recorded a number of the problems he had encountered:

Five times I received from the Jews the forty lashes minus one. Three times I was beaten with rods, once I was stoned, three times I was shipwrecked, I spent a night and a day in the open sea, I have been constantly on the move. I have been in danger from rivers, in danger from bandits, in danger from my own countrymen, in danger from Gentiles; in danger in the city, in danger in the country, in danger at sea; and in danger from false brothers. I have labored and toiled and have often gone without sleep; I have known hunger and thirst and have often gone without food; I have been cold and naked. Besides everything else, I face daily the pressure of my concern for all the churches (11:24-28).

Yes, Paul knew the frustration and discouragement associated with problems and failures. But he saw God faithfully take him through all those negative experiences; this enabled him to become an overcomer. Through his problems, trials, and failures he had learned that, "I can do everything God asks me to with the help of Christ who gives me the strength and power" (Phil. 4:13, TLB).

Therefore, take advantage of your failures. See them as opportunities to learn how to become an overcomer. You only have two choices: You can become an overcomer, or you can let your failures overcome you. I don't know about you, but I intend to side with Paul!

God's Plan: To Turn Our Failures into Success

God never promised Christians that our lives would be free from failure. He did, however, promise that if we love Him and seek His purpose for our lives, He will turn all our failures into success. Paul affirms this fact by telling us, "And we know that in all things God works for the good of those who love Him, who have been called according to His purpose" (Rom. 8:28).

This is a fantastic verse. God says that in *all* things (which includes our failures as well as our successes), God promises to work the situations for *our good* if we love Him and are putting Him first in our lives. That means that no matter how bad the situation may look at present, God will make it turn out for our good and benefit.

The truth of this promise is illustrated in the story of Joseph. As you may recall, Joseph's brothers did not like him because they felt their father cared more for Joseph than for them. So the young man's brothers sold him to a caravan of Ishmaelites who, in turn, sold him as a slave in Egypt (Gen. 3:7).

Even though Joseph's brothers acted out of hate and resentment, God brought good out of this situation—both for Joseph *and* his brothers. After Joseph arrived in Egypt and became a slave, God used a series of events to take him out of slavery; eventually, he became second in command over all Egypt (Gen. 39—41).

Then a severe famine developed in the land; Joseph's father sent his sons to Egypt to buy grain. When the brothers discovered that Joseph was an important Egyptian official, they were afraid he would kill them for their earlier treachery. Yet Joseph explained to his siblings that even though they had tried to harm him, God meant it for good. God had used that situation to save Joseph's family from the terrible famine (Gen. 41—45).

Why God Allows Failures

Have you ever heard someone say, "If God really loved me, He wouldn't have let this happen"? I have to admit that there have been many times when I've wondered why God let me fail, or why a certain problem developed.

Fortunately, the Book of Deuteronomy sheds some light on this question:

> Remember how the Lord your God led you all the way in the desert these forty years, to humble you and to test you in order to know what was in your heart, whether or not you would keep His commands" (8:2).

Usually when we think of God leading us, we envision being led "through green pastures." However, notice that in this verse, God led His people into the desert. He led them into a hot, dry, barren wasteland where there was neither food nor water. He *could* have led them through a paradise where there was plenty of food and water. But He didn't.

Sure enough, it didn't take long before the Children of Israel displayed their true colors. They were barely out of the shadows of the city before they started complaining that Moses had led them out to be killed. When the going got tough, they wanted to run back to Egypt and again submit themselves to Pharaoh; they weren't willing to trust God to solve their problems.

Now look at this verse again. Why did God lead Israel into this difficult situation? Wasn't it to humble them, to test them in order to know what was in their hearts? The fact is, God wanted to know if they would still love Him and keep His commandments when the chips were down and the pressure was on.

If God had led the people through green, watered valleys where there was an abundance of food and no problems, the people would not have had to trust God to meet their needs. They could have made it on their own.

The same holds true for us as business people. As long as things are going great—our sales are up, customers are happy, and we aren't having any problems with our employees—it is easy to run the company without trusting God for help. But, when sales stop, orders are canceled, and the cash flow ceases (but bills keep coming in), then God finds out how much we *really* believe Him and His Word.

Satan's Objective When You Fail

When we fail, God wants us to trust Him so that He can save us from our troubles. He then wants us to tell people that He was responsible for our rescue. Yet in the same situation, Satan wants to make us bitter, resentful, fearful, and angry toward God for our problems.

In short, God uses failures to build us up. Satan uses failures to tear us down.

As soon as we fail, Satan goes on the offensive. The first place he attacks is our attitudes. He tries to poison our minds with all types of negative thoughts. Remember Raymond Sutton? As he saw failure approaching, he became hostile toward God, the people with whom he worked, the people at the bank, and even his wife. Almost all his thought patterns were negative.

That is exactly what Satan wants! If he can turn us against God, we certainly won't be trusting Him to solve our problems; we will be relying on our *own* abilities.

How to Protect Your Attitude
Because Satan tries to turn our attitudes from positive to negative when failures come, our question should be, "How can I maintain a positive attitude in the face of failure?"

The first step is to submit yourself to God. James' epistle tells us, "Submit yourselves, then, to God. Resist the devil, and he will flee from you" (4:7). We must submit the negative situation to God and realize that by doing so, God will work the situation out for our good (Rom. 8:28).

Next, we must resist Satan's attempts to focus our thoughts on "negatives," and to develop bitterness and resentment.

Then, we must begin thanking God in the midst of our difficult situations. That doesn't mean we necessarily have to be thankful *for* the situations. But we need to be thanking God *during* this trial, because we know that God will rescue us from times of trouble (Ps. 50:15). In essence, our attitudes should reflect Paul's instructions to the Thessalonians:

Always be joyful. Always keep on praying. No matter what happens, always be thankful, for this is God's will for you who belong to Christ Jesus

(1 Thes. 5:16-18, TLB).

Finally, we must force ourselves to dwell on the positive aspects of the situation, rather than on its negative dimensions. Whether we want to admit it or not, we *are* in control of our attitudes. We allow our thoughts to be positive or negative.

It is true that sometimes our "normal reaction" might be to focus on the negative. As Christians, however, we should seek to dwell on the positive. As the Apostle counseled:

Fix your thoughts on what is true and good and right. Think about things that are pure and lovely, and dwell on the fine, good things in others. Think about all you can praise God for and be glad about" (Phil. 4:8, TLB).

The choice is up to you. You can dwell on all the negative things which Satan is trying to shove into your mind, you can become a prisoner to fear, you can allow your potential for further success to diminish. Or you can listen to God and the promises He makes to rescue us and turn our failures into something good. If we listen to God, it will be easier to think on the positive things listed in Philippians 4:8.

As for me, I am learning from experience that it is far better to focus on the positive things that will come out of my failures as I submit myself to God. I know I will continue to have failures in my life and business. But I'm also glad to know that such setbacks will only be stepping-stones on the way to success.

Chapter Summary
All of us experience failure; our failures, however, can be keys to future success. God promises that if we trust Him during

our times of failure, He will rescue us. All He asks in return is that we give Him the credit (Ps. 50:15).

According to James, a lot of good can come out of our failures; therefore, we should remain positive when they occur (1:2-4). Failures committed to God will help build our characters and maturity, and give us confidence in God's ability to solve our problems.

Scripture states that the person who is trusting God during a problem or failure doesn't need to worry; God will work the situation out for our good. His plan, then, is to turn our failures into success for the future.

Satan's goal when we fail, however, is to turn us away from God and make us bitter and resentful. He wants to make us fearful so we will be unwilling to try again. As a result, we miss out on the full potential and blessing God has for us.

When failures come, it is important that we monitor our attitudes. We must remain positive, believing that God will rescue us and turn the situation into good. James tells us to submit ourselves to God. By resisting Satan we will find him fleeing from us (4:7). This is the first step toward insuring that our attitudes remain positive. Next, we must thank God during the situation (1 Thes. 5:16-18). Finally, we must make a decision to focus on the positive aspects of the negative situation (Phil. 4:8).

Personal Application

1. If you currently are going through a problem or failure, or if you have gone through one recently, evaluate the apparent cause of that failure.
2. Review Psalm 50:15; Romans 8:28; James 1:2-4; and Philippians 4:8.

    a. What are the promises listed in these passages concerning what God will do for us when failures come?

    b. What conditions must we meet to receive these promises?

    c. How should these passages be applied when failures occur?

    d. What things tend to hinder us from applying these promises?

9
Dealing with Stress
in Business

On a flight from Dallas to Denver, I sat next to an industrial psychologist who worked as a consultant for some of the nation's largest electronics companies. Her main area of professional interest was in the field of stress management. I'll never forget the conversation we had.

"Stress among business people in the United States is becoming a major problem," she told me. "And it will probably get worse before it gets better." I asked her why she thought that was true.

"The pressures on business people today are greater than ever before," she replied. "The unstable economy, increased competition, foreign manufacturers, and the faster pace of society have all contributed to a phenomenal buildup of stress on people. To give you some indication of just how widespread stress is," she continued, "there are over 60 million anti-stress tablets consumed annually in this country."

Before we landed in Denver, she mentioned that more and more companies are becoming aware of the problems associated with stress. For the past year she had not been able to keep up with the demand for her services.

The True Source of Stress and Anxiety

While preparing this chapter, I made a trip to my local library to see what the "experts" on stress management had to say about the subject. I was surprised to find that the library carried over 100 books on the topic of stress. Almost all the ones I reviewed discussed the "causes" of stress and anxiety: overwork, financial worries, fear of the unknown, poor relationships, and various unmet needs.

After completing my study of the secular views of the causes of stress, I turned to the Bible to see what it had to say on the subject. I have to admit that I was surprised at the number of passages dealing with anxiety and stress. Scripture discusses in detail the "cause" and "effect" of stress—and gives a step-by-step procedure for eliminating it.

To understand the true source of stress and anxiety, then, we first need to look at two passages—one in Exodus, the other in Hebrews.

The Book of Exodus notes that the people of Israel, under Moses' leadership, left the Sihn Desert and came to Rephidim (17:1, TLB). But once there, they couldn't find any water. As a result, the Israelites became very angry with both God and Moses, whom they accused of bringing the entire Israelite nation out to the desert to die of thirst (17:2-3). In fact, they went so far as to ask, "Is Jehovah going to take care of us or not?" (17:7, TLB)

Consider their question: *"Is Jehovah going to take care of us or not?"* These people doubted God's ability to meet their needs. When the Israelites found themselves with a problem they were unable to handle, they refused to believe God and to trust Him to solve it for them.

Consequently, fear overtook them and they developed anxiety over the situation. But God soon supernaturally supplied water for all the people. By doing so, He proved to them that they didn't need to worry when they ran into situations they couldn't solve. If they would just trust Him in their times of need, He would always take care of them. Their sources of anxiety would be eliminated.

In the Book of Hebrews, God recounts this experience. He points out that this generation of Israelites never got to enter the "rest" of the Promised Land. Why? Because they would not put their faith in Him in their times of need (Heb. 3—4).

In ensuing verses, God gives us a warning. He tells us to not be like the Israelites who failed to trust Him in their time of need. For if we mirror their behavior, peace and rest will elude us too (3:15-19; 4:3-7).

What are the implications of these two passages? Simply this: *Failure to trust God during our times of need is the true source of stress and anxiety.*

The secular world identifies overwork, financial worries, and a fear of the unknown as the roots of stress. But in actuality, such things are the *effects* of not trusting God to meet our needs—they are not the *causes* of anxiety.

What Happens When We Don't Trust God to Meet Our Needs?

As mentioned earlier, the world's "experts" on stress management have mistakenly identified the effects of stress for its causes. And God's Word tells us that stress and anxiety occur as a result of our not trusting the Lord to totally meet our needs in any situation.

Thus, once we conclude that God is not going to meet our needs, we assume it's all up to us. We'll have to solve our problems ourselves. The world's philosophy is: *If it's going to be... it's up to me!* That catchy little phrase—which sounds so inspiring and logical on the surface—actually is at the very heart of Humanism and the "New Age" movement.

It says that if a problem is going to be solved, "I" have to solve it. If a need is going to be met, "I" have to meet it. It says that *all* solutions are the result of "my" resourcefulness. And it's exactly the way most business people operate in the marketplace today.

Once I buy into this philosophy, though, and start assuming that the solution to a problem must come from somewhere within me, the next step is for me to begin working *harder* and *smarter.* Since my destiny is "up to me," I'll need to start working ten hours a day at the office instead of eight. And six days a week instead of five. Yet when that doesn't solve the problem, my next reaction is to become fearful that I might fail.

My fears then create tension, worry, and anxiety. These emotions build up inside me and lead to stress.

When the world's experts look at me in this anxious state, they conclude that my stress is the result of overwork. Yet in truth, my problem is a spiritual one. I failed to trust God to meet my need. I assumed that the only one who could meet the need was me. And that's when the chain of events I outlined above commenced; my fear produced anxieties that led to emotional stress. But it all started with my failure to trust

God! My stress was a *symptom* of the spiritual problem of not trusting God.

The psalmist notes, "It is in vain that you rise up early and go late to rest, eating the bread of anxious toil; for He gives to His beloved sleep" (127:2, RSV). God is telling us here that "His beloved"—those who trust Him—will have rest and sleep. On the other hand, He is claiming that individuals who rise early and go to bed late because they are trying to manage their problems on their own, will wind up eating the fruit of anxiety and stress. Likewise, when the Lord says that "It is in vain" that we pursue such activities, He is pointing out that we are actually accomplishing very little for all our efforts. We would accomplish a lot more in a lot less time if we would trust God instead of ourselves.

The Physical Effects of Stress

Dr. Lester Henderson, a medical doctor specializing in family practice once told me, "Stress and its side effects keep me in business." He indicated that at least 75 percent of his patients come to him suffering from the results of stress and its effects on their bodies. He mentioned that in most cases, heart attacks, high blood pressure, strokes, and ulcers could be traced directly to the problems of stress and anxiety.

Dr. Henderson went on to say that stress and worry also were the root causes of obesity. "If we could remove stress and worry from people's lives," he told me, "many of their weight problems would take care of themselves." He explained that stress-induced nervousness often caused people to become excessive eaters.

At this point, it would be wise to review Jesus' observation that, "The thief's purpose is to steal, kill, and destroy. My

purpose is to give life in all its fullness" (John 10:10, TLB).
Satan's purpose is to kill and destroy. One of the ways in which he literally accomplishes this task is to get people to believe his deceptive philosophy, "If it's to be ... it's up to me." His goal is to persuade us to trust ourselves in our times of need, rather than to rely on God. In doing so, though, we develop worry, anxiety, and stress, which in turn lead to all kinds of physical problems and sickness—even death.

But notice too that Christ said He came to "give life in all its fullness." He wants us to place our trust in Him, not only for eternal life, but also for all our needs in our businesses. As we do this, we will experience the calmness, joy, and peace that come with *true* success.

As the Apostle Paul said, "I can do everything God asks me to with the help of Christ who gives me the strength and power" (Phil. 4:13, TLB). A knowledge of this fact allowed Paul to live in stressful situations without being overcome by stress.

Why Do We Try to Solve Our Own Problems?
Dr. Lester Henderson also told me that he has observed that business people tend to have more problems with stress and anxiety than do other people. It isn't necessarily because their jobs are filled with more problems and pressures. It's because business people—and particularly business owners—tend to be more *independent* than other people.

In our society, we have made a hero out of the *self-made* man. The person who makes it to the top of the ladder by dint of his own ingenuity and willpower is greatly admired and respected by most people. And, of course, the self-made man needs to be independent; he must take risks and assume responsibliity for both failures and successes.

But in Jeremiah we read: "The Lord says: 'Cursed is the man who puts his trust in mortal man and turns his heart away from God'" (17:5, TLB). This verse makes it clear that God sees no virtue in a person's being "self-made." In fact, the Lord says that the man who believes his own business acumen accounts for his success is cursed.

Granted, if a person is going to succeed in business, he needs to be bright, aggressive, and shrewd. These same traits are serious weaknesses, however, when it comes to learning how to humble oneself before God. They're a hindrance to trusting Him with our businesses' futures. Believe me; as a businessman, I speak from experience.

I frequently find myself saying, "God, You just tell me what You want done. Then step aside, and I'll go take care of it." But God says, "No, Myron. I'll tell you what I want done. But I expect you to trust *Me* to do it through you."

Speaking through the Prophet Isaiah, the Lord said, "This is the one I esteem: he who is humble and contrite in spirit, and trembles at My word" (66:2). Yet the marketplace says: "This is the one I esteem: he who is strong-willed, tough-minded, fights the odds, and makes it on his own."

In short, God honors those who adore Him—the world honors those who ignore Him.

As business people, we must learn that we can't deal with God in the same way that we "deal" in the marketplace. God isn't impressed with our independence, willpower, or raw courage. He looks favorably on people who will allow Him to be Lord of their lives. And for Him to be our Lord, we must be His servants.

I like all the benefits that accompany Christ's being my Lord. But I must admit I'm not too crazy about all the stuff that comes with the servant part. A servant must always be submissive to his master and lord. The fact is, though, that you and I as Christian business people *must* learn to be God's servants if we are going to make Him Lord of our marketplace. And to do that, we must first learn humility.

To learn humility, I have to recognize that I desperately need God. I can't manage a business on my own. I don't have all the answers. I do blow it regularly. And I will never achieve what God wants for my life without His constant help.

I must confess that despite my knowledge of these truths, like most business people I know, I still have problems with submission. *That* is why many of us have problems with stress and anxiety. We are unsuccessfully trying to do for ourselves what God already has promised to do for us. Remember Psalm 50:15? In it, God said, "I want you to trust Me in your times of trouble, so I can rescue you, and you can give Me glory" (TLB).

Hey, folks! Let's stop fooling ourselves. Let's humble ourselves before God and trust Him. He wants to rescue us; all we have to do is give Him the credit. That certainly seems like a reasonable request on His part; after all, don't most businessmen ask you to "tell a friend" if you like their products?

Besides, when I trust God to solve my problems, not only does He handle my dilemmas, but I get to stop worrying about them! And that is the key to freeing myself from stress. So I get a free bonus on the side just for "letting" God work in my behalf. You can't beat a deal like that!

How to Get Rid of Stress

As we've seen throughout this chapter, if you are experiencing stress and anxiety in a certain situation, it is because you have not submitted that situation to God, humbled yourself before Him, and trusted Him to work His will.

The way to get rid of stress, therefore, is to make Jesus Christ Lord of your life in each situation. And don't make Him Lord of your life once and then go about your business, assuming that He will automatically sanction everything you plan to do. You make Jesus Lord by letting Him *be* Lord—that is, by giving Him control of each situation in your business dealings. This can be achieved by following the steps listed below:

(1) *Examine yourself and the problem situation; confess any sin that may be in your life.* In following this step, pray as David did when he said, "Search me, O God, and know my heart; test me and know my anxious thoughts. See if there is any offensive way in me, and lead me in the way everlasting" (Ps. 124:23-24).

Like David, we must ask God to search our lives and motives. Then as He points out our sins, we must confess them to God, asking His forgiveness (1 John 1:9).

(2) *Next, you must submit yourself to God, asking that His will take precedence over your will.* In Luke's Gospel, Jesus tells us that "Anyone who wants to follow Me must put aside his own desires and conveniences and carry his cross with him every day and keep close to Me!" (9:23, TLB) Jesus Christ expects us to put aside our plans and expectations, and to put Him *first* in every situation!

(3) *Ask God to direct you in your decisions and plans.* God wants to make a direct contribution to our planning and decision-making. "I will instruct you," says the Lord, "and guide you along the best pathway for your life; I will advise you and watch your progress" (Ps. 32:8, TLB). Once we

ask God for direction, we must be willing to let Him do the directing.

(4) *Be at peace with God in whatever He wants you to do.* If we really are committed to serving God and doing His will, then we will want to please Him. That means we will be eager to obey Him. We will not resent His will or complain about obeying His Word. Scripture puts it this way: "Submit to God and be at peace with Him; in this way prosperity will come to you" (Job 22:21).

(5) *Thank God for what He has already done, and for what He is going to do in the future.* In his first letter to the church at Thessalonica, Paul says, "No matter what happens, always be thankful, for this is God's will for you who belong to Christ Jesus" (5:18, TLB). It is God's will that we be thankful in every situation. However, we can't be thankful *and* worry about things at the same time. Thus, God not only wants us to be thankful, but He instructs us to be at peace with ourselves and with Him.

(6) *Finally, pray about every situation, committing the five steps above to God as you talk to Him.* We are told in Philippians:

Don't worry about anything; instead, pray about everything; tell God your needs and don't forget to thank Him for His answers. If you do this you will experience God's peace, which is far more wonderful than the human mind can understand. His peace will keep your thoughts and your hearts quiet and at rest as you trust in Christ Jesus (4:6-7, TLB).

What a great passage! These verses give us the key to living a life that's free from anxiety, worry, and stress. Instead of wondering how we are going to solve our problems, this passage points out that we are to take them to God, telling Him our needs. Once we do this, we are to thank Him ahead of time for the answer that is coming.

If we follow these guidelines, God will fill our hearts and minds with the peace and assurance that He is in control. His answer already is being worked out. It's on the way according to His plan and timetable.

I can speak from experience: Every time I apply these principles, God not only removes my stress and gives me peace, but His solutions are always far better than anything I could have accomplished on my own!

Chapter Summary

Stress among business people has become a major problem. It not only effects us personally, but it affects the performance of our businesses. In addition, and most importantly, it greatly hinders our relationships with God.

Stress occurs when we try to solve our own problems—and then realize we don't have all the answers. As a result, we become frustrated, worried, and anxious. We wind up working harder and longer trying to solve our problems; instead, we should be turning them over to God and trusting Him to solve them. Thus, stress is the result of a spiritual problem. It is not due to overwork, financial problems, etc.

Stress causes numerous physical illnesses, including heart problems, high blood pressure, strokes, and obesity. It makes us tired, irritable, and short-tempered.

Christian business people sometimes find it difficult to trust God to solve their problems; they are accustomed to being independent, strong-willed individualists who take care of their own needs. This is why business people frequently have problems with stress. They believe the maxim, "If it's to be...it's up to me." However, such a philosophy leads to stress and anxiety.

To get rid of stress, we must be willing to confess that our self-centered, independent nature is sinful. We must submit ourselves to God, asking that His will be done in our lives. Then we must ask God to direct us in all our decisions and plans. We must be willing to do what He says instead of what we want. We also must thank Him for being willing to solve our problems and meet our needs.

The key passage to apply in dealing with stress is Philippians 4:6-7:

> Don't worry about anything; instead, pray about everything; tell God your needs and don't forget to thank Him for His answers. If you do this you will experience God's peace, which is far more wonderful than the human mind can understand. His peace will keep your thoughts and your hearts quiet and at rest as you trust in Christ Jesus" (TLB).

Personal Application

1. Do you feel that you are worrying and anxious about situations in your business, or in other areas of life? If so, what exactly are you trying to do or solve on your own? Read Psalm 50:15 and commit the issue to God.

2. Review the section on "How to Get Rid of Stress." If any problems are worrying you, follow the six steps outlined in this section.

10
How to Avoid
Personal "Burnout"

BURNOUT! When I hear that term my mind paints a vivid picture of a once-beautiful building's charred, crumbled, skeletal remains. But I see another vision, one of business people I've known who've experienced the disaster of *emotional burnout.*

Emotional burnout can take a highly enthusiastic, energetic, productive person and leave him devastated, demoralized, and devoid of the motivation that once propelled him to success. Burnout can be defined as a type of job-related stress which is often caused by constant interaction with people and their problems. Emotional exhaustion typically is part of burnout.

This phenomenon is most prevalent among individuals who have extensive "people contact" jobs, or who are high achievers—profiles that fit many executives, salespeople, and other business persons.

Two Burnout Case Studies

The Bible gives us some classic case studies concerning burnout and how it develops. In fact, some of the greatest spiritual leaders of the Old Testament suffered from this condition. Among them were Moses, and Jeremiah. Each was a cornerstone of spiritual leadership in his day. Each accomplished great things for God. And both had one thing in common: they worked closely with people—perhaps *too* closely.

Moses. Moses is one of the best-known figures in Scripture. He is generally credited with writing the first five books of the Old Testament, and was charged with the awesome task of leading the Children of Israel out of Egypt into the Promised Land.

However, despite his achievements, this great spiritual and political leader provides us with one of the most vivid examples of burnout on record.

Let's pick up our case study of Moses as recorded in Exodus 18. In this chapter, Jethro, Moses' father-in-law, came to visit. While there, he observed how Moses was constantly dealing with the people, trying to solve their problems and answer their questions. Moses' routine bothered Jethro:

> The next day Moses sat as usual to hear the people's complaints against each other, from morning to evening. When Moses' father-in-law saw how much time this was taking, he said, "Why are you trying to do all this alone, with people standing here all day long to get your help?" (Ex. 18:13-14, TLB)

Jethro's question was a perceptive one. He realized that constant contact with these people ultimately could prove harmful to Moses. After all, Moses supervised the people, met with them, and listened to their complaints and disagreements. He tried to solve their problems to the best of his ability. And as we soon shall see, this arrangement eventually *did* produce some serious problems for Moses.

Now let's move on to Exodus 32. In this chapter, we find Moses on Mt. Sinai, meeting with God. Yet at the same time, the people of Israel—led by Aaron, Moses' brother—were making a golden calf and worshiping it.

When God saw what the people were doing, He was extremely angry. He told Moses,

> I have seen what a stubborn, rebellious lot these
> people are. Now let Me alone and My anger shall
> blaze out against them and destroy them all; and I
> will make you, Moses, into a great nation instead of
> them" (32:9-10, TLB).

But Moses begged God to reconsider His decision and the Lord spared the people. At this point in Moses' life he was willing to stick up for the people and to tolerate them, even when they forsook God and worshiped a golden calf.

As time went by, Moses continued to work extensively with the people. He designed their worship ceremonies. He built the ark and the tabernacle and designed the latter's furnishings. He instituted religious offerings the people were to present. He established health regulations, judicial statutes, and social codes. Then he undertook the mammoth task of numbering all the tribes of the nation.

One day, though, the people started complaining to Moses about not having meat to eat. They were tired of eating the manna God had been providing. Moses became very angry, threw up his hands and appeared ready to throw in the towel:

> Moses said to the Lord, "Why pick on me, to give

me the burden of a people like this? Are they *my* children? Am I their father? Is that why You have given me the job of nursing them along like babies until we get to the land You promised their ancestors? Where am I supposed to get meat for all these people? . . . I can't carry this nation by myself! The load is far too heavy! If You are going to treat me like this, please kill me right now; it will be a kindness! Let me out of this impossible situation!" (Num. 11:11-15, TLB)

Clearly, these sound like the words of a burned-out person! Moses simply had spent too much time trying to please too many people. Now his body and mind were shouting, "Enough!"

Jeremiah. Like Moses, Jeremiah had an extensive "people contact" job. God had called Jeremiah to be a prophet "to the nations" (1:5). So he constantly was working with people, trying to get them to listen to God, turn from their sin, and obey His Word.

But, this prophet also had trouble with the people for whom he was responsible. It is worthwhile to quote one of Jeremiah's laments at length:

O Lord, You deceived me when You promised me Your help. I have to give them Your messages because You are stronger than I am, but now I am the laughingstock of the city, mocked by all. You have never once let me speak a word of kindness to them; always it is disaster and horror and destruction. No wonder they scoff and mock and make my name a household joke. And I can't quit! For if I say I'll never again mention the Lord—never more speak in His name—then His word in my heart is like fire that burns in my bones, and I can't hold it in any longer. Yet on every side I hear their whispered threats, and am afraid. "We will report you," they say. Even those who were my friends are watching me, waiting for a fatal slip.... Cursed be the day that I was born!... Oh, that I had died within my mother's womb, that it had been my grave! Why was I ever born? For my life has been but trouble and sorrow and shame (Jer. 20:7-18, TLB).

We have just looked at two of the Old Testament's greatest leaders. They were spiritual giants. They walked with God. They were committed to carrying out His plan for their lives. Yet both of them experienced severe emotional burnout. You may be asking yourself, "How could that happen?" In the remaining sections of this chapter, we'll try to answer that question. We'll also seek to identify the symptoms of burnout and suggest ways to help people recover from—and prevent—it.

What Causes Burnout?

Burnout, as mentioned earlier, is most prevalent among high achievers and people in the "helping" services. Business people generally are high achievers, and Christians usually are concerned about helping people. This combination makes Christian business people prime candidates for burnout.

In examining the subject of burnout, we must realize that we are dealing with people's emotions. Since no two people are alike, we all react differently to stress. Consequently, it would be a mistake to try to say that *one factor* is the prime cause of burnout. Specific "patterns" *are* evidenced in most cases of burnout, however.

In the space allotted for this chapter, we will not be able to discuss all these patterns. We *will,* however, consider ones that are most important. As we do, we will look at how they led to burnout in our two earlier case studies—Moses and Jeremiah.

(1) *We try to do everything by ourselves.* We've established that burnout occurs most often among high achievers. And high achievers frequently are independent, loners. They usually would rather complete a task themselves than take the time to ask someone else to help. This was true with Moses. As Exodus indicates, he "sat *as usual* to hear the people's complaints... from morning to evening" (18:13, TLB; italics mine).

For Moses, this responsibility had become habitual. The fact that he failed to delegate his chores to others only compounded his problems. These two factors helped contribute to his eventual burnout.

If, as a business person, you are trying to manage your affairs all by yourself, you too may be on the road to burnout, just like Moses.

(2) *Our accomplishments don't meet our expectations.* Since we are trying to "do it all," we often get bogged down with details. Therefore, dealing with people becomes frustrating; their problems represent just one more thing that contributes to our getting farther behind.

Because high achievers are goal-oriented, when people and situations hinder us from accomplishing our goals; we get frustrated and unhappy. At first our frustration is directed toward the people we consider barriers to the achievement of our goals. Later, that frustration is transferred to our jobs; eventually, it will be directed toward ourselves.

(3) *We lose proper perspective—molehills become mountains.* Our frustrations and dissatisfactions with people, our jobs, and ourselves often will cause us to lose a sense of perspective. In essence, we start losing touch with reality.

In a passage we considered earlier, Moses was willing to forgive the people for worshiping the golden calf. However, when the people later asked for meat, Moses' reaction bordered on the irrational. He told God, "I can't carry this nation by myself! The load is far too heavy! If You are going to treat me like this, please kill me right now; it will be a kindness! Let me out of this impossible situation!" (Num. 11:14-15, TLB)

At that point, Moses was totally burned-out concerning his job as leader of Israel. He wanted nothing more to do with these people, his job, or even his own life.

This was the man who had held out his staff and the Red Sea parted; struck a rock and water came out of it; received the Ten Commandments from God on Mt. Sinai. But now the people were asking for a little thing like meat and he was ready to quit! What a classic example of how we act and react when burnout occurs. We are no longer capable of handling the smallest incidents. Molehills become mountains.

(4) *As Christians, we think we can't let God down.* This is one of the major causes of burnout among dedicated Christians. We are committed to God and His great

work. Yet because we try to do everything ourselves, we feel the weight of responsibility to "make it happen for God."

Moses was caught in this mental trap. God told him that He would supply the people with nothing but meat for a whole month. Yet when Moses heard God make this promise, he seemed incredulous. Consider his words:

If we butcher all our flocks and herds it won't be enough! We would have to catch every fish in the ocean to fulfill Your promise! (Num. 11:22, TLB)

In effect, Moses was implying that *he* would have to help God keep His promise to Israel. He was taking God's responsibility onto his own shoulders!

Many Christians are guilty of doing the same thing. In their enthusiasm to see God's work accomplished, they try to do it all themselves. This is a sure way to burn yourself out in a job. Even though we may be high achievers and love God dearly, we can't always do His work for Him. In fact, we shouldn't even try.

God didn't tell Moses to supply the meat. God said *He* would provide it. And He did (Num. 11:23-25). Shouldn't we have confidence in this God?

(5) *We conclude that it is impossible to accomplish the job, so we begin to hate what we're doing.* Burnout occurs when we decide that it's impossible to accomplish the task set before us. This conclusion frequently is made when other people fail to respond favorably to us and what we are doing. For the salesperson, burnout often comes when he concludes, "It's impossible to sell this product. No one wants it. No one will ever buy

it. It is priced far too high." And the excuses go on and on. As a result, such people start to hate their products, their jobs, the company they work for—and usually even themselves, for failing.

Jeremiah was a classic example in this category. As we saw earlier, he got very bent out of shape at God (Jer. 20:7-8). Because of his bad experiences, Jeremiah concluded that it was impossible to get the people to listen to his message.

Jeremiah's conclusion was the same as Moses'. The job just wasn't worth the effort, the goal could not be achieved. As a result, both men wound up hating their jobs and themselves.

Burnout is an evolving process. It may take anywhere from one to twenty years to develop, depending on the individual and the circumstances of his job. Yet one thing *is* certain: We are on the road to burnout when we try to manage tasks all by ourselves. When we fall into that trap, it isn't long until our accomplishments don't keep up with our expectations. This then creates emotional pressure on us; we begin losing perspective—molehills suddenly become mountains.

As Christians, we also think we can't let God down, so we work harder to please Him. But we wind up trying to do His job for Him. We finally conclude that it's impossible to accomplish the job, so we begin hating it—and ourselves.

At this point we want to run. We want to give up on people, the job, ourselves—and unfortunately—sometimes on God.

How to Identify the Symptoms of Burnout
Burnout is more prevalent in the United States than in many other countries because of our high orientation to competi-

tion, achievement, and success. As stated earlier, high achievers are the most frequent victims of burnout.

As a management consultant I have had an opportunity to meet and work with numerous people on their way to, in the middle of, and on their way out of burnout. I've gone through this painful process myself. So I speak from the position of a participant as well as that of an observer.

Burnout has many symptoms. They include the following:

(1) *People experiencing burn-out are very irritable.* A burnout victim's nerves are on edge. The smallest incident can touch off a giant emotional explosion. We saw that happening with both Moses and Jeremiah. They greatly overreacted when confronted with problem situations.

(2) *They are emotionally exhausted.* Employees suffering from burnout have no emotional energy left. They suddenly are unable to cope with events and situations that they once would have taken in stride. For example, I once had a secretary who was experiencing burnout. She had been an executive secretary for twenty-five years and was very good at what she did. But her job eventually lost its challenge. (As a young supervisor, I must confess that I didn't know how to effectively use a secretary of her caliber. Part of her problem, then, was my fault.) One day I walked into her office area and found her crying. She had misplaced a roll of Scotch tape and couldn't find it.

Normally, losing Scotch tape is not that big a deal. But to someone who is experiencing burnout, something this insignificant can touch off a crisis with which he or she can't cope.

(3) *Their emotional exhaustion leads to physical exhaustion.* People experiencing burnout are constantly tired. They not only are drained emotionally, but physically, as well. Thus they lack both the emotional and physical energy needed to do their jobs.

(4) *They can no longer see things objectively.* Jeremiah accused God of deceiving him (Jer. 20:7). Under normal circumstances, Jeremiah would never have dreamed of saying something like that. But under the influence of burnout, his objectivity was diminished.

(5) *Their decisions tend to be made on the basis of feelings.* Once people lose objectivity, they rely heavily on emotions and feelings for guidance. As a result, they become unpredictable—doing things that are totally out of character for them.

(6) *They lose their courage, sense of identity, and self-worth.* This occurs when employees can't believe that strong, motivated, goal-oriented achievers like themselves are going through a difficult experience. They no longer "know" themselves or what they are capable of doing.

(7) *They no longer will take risks.* The person experiencing burnout believes he is a failure. He is in emotional shock because of that realization. Therefore he no longer will take any risks; he wants to make sure that he doesn't fail again.

(8) *Eventually, they give up on life itself.* Burnout victims may not actually commit suicide, but the thought of doing so crosses their minds. Both Moses and Jeremiah expressed a wish to die. Likewise, persons experiencing burnout also "give up." They conclude they will

never succeed at anything again. In fact, they may be convinced that they aren't capable of accomplishing *anything*.

(9) *If Christians, they may get angry at God and blame Him for their problems.* This response tends to be a result of the victim's emotional and physical exhaustion. As a person's strength drains, he has a tendency to stop reading and studying God's Word, and spending time with the Lord in prayer. As a result, his relationship with God deteriorates. Satan tries to use this series of events to turn the person against God by getting him to blame the Lord for all his problems.

How to Help People Recover from Burnout

Burnout doesn't just "wear off." Specific steps *must* be taken to help people recover from its effects.

(1) *People must have time away from the job.* It is the day-to-day activities associated with one's job that cause burnout. Therefore, to begin recovering from burnout, people must have some time away from their places of work. This is *not* just an option. It is the first step toward recovery.

The person experiencing burnout must have a change of environment and be removed—at least temporarily—from the surroundings that produced the problems. The smart supervisor or business owner will pay for this time away and not deduct it from regular vacation time. He will also see to it that the place to which the employee goes is conducive to rest and relaxation.

(2) *This "time-away" period must not be used for "self-*

evaluation." The purpose of this vacation period is to remove the employee from the tensions that initially caused his burnout and to encourage him to rest and relax physically. Earlier, we pointed out that in the burnout process, people become both emotionally and physically exhausted. Thus, employees must begin recovering from physical exhaustion before they can recover from mental and emotional exhaustion.

They must be instructed, therefore, to avoid an exhaustive self-evaluation of their problems at this time. Such analysis can come later.

(3) *They must start a physical exercise program.* People experiencing burnout are under a great deal of stress, which invariably increases their blood pressure and pulse rates. Therefore, they must become involved in some type of physical exercise program to restore their health. In many instances, it will be necessary to consult a physician at this point to insure that overexertion does not occur. Remember: these people have been high achievers and usually undertake any new program or challenge with great gusto; yet they must not be allowed to overdo an exercise regimen.

(4) *When they return to work, their jobs must include new responsibilities.* Returning employees may not find themselves faced by completely new jobs, but their old ones must be sufficiently redesigned to incorporate new duties and responsibilities. In other words, a short vacation and interesting exercise program will not reverse burnout. We must keep in mind that it was the activities and circumstances associated with a particular job that originally produced burnout. Consequently,

we must alter the functions of this job—at least to some degree.

(5) *They must experience immediate success.* People who are burned-out have been experiencing one failure after the other—at least in their minds. Therefore, it is imperative that they begin experiencing immediate success in order to restore their confidence. The supervisor of a person recovering from burnout must design a series of short-range goals that the employee can achieve within the course of no more than a week.

Jim Ander, a former business partner and close friend of mine, has helped numerous people recover from burnout. He once told me, "When people return to work from their time away, I make sure they experience success within the first couple of days—even if it's nothing more than beating me at a game of tennis. They have to begin learning again that they can succeed."

(6) *They must develop a new purpose for their lives.* The employer who is helping an individual recover from burnout must realize that the employee's whole purpose in life may have been destroyed. Remember, Moses and Jeremiah were ready to give up on life itself.

The burnout victim must be encouraged to develop long-term goals that will help give new meaning and purpose to life. Fulfillment of short-term goals will help rebuild the confidence your employee needs to achieve these future goals. This, in turn, will help instill a sense of purpose to his life and work.

You must keep in mind that burnout doesn't just affect one's job. It ultimately changes all of life—family, hobbies, friends, and special interests. Therefore, all areas of the employee's life must be dealt with and, in some cases, rebuilt.

(7) *The person with burnout must become accountable to someone.* Overcoming burnout does not happen automatically. As the steps outlined above are implemented, someone must become responsible to see that they are carried out. Accordingly, the person with burnout must be willing to submit himself to an individual (usually a supervisor or trained counselor), and become accountable to that person for application and follow-through of this recovery plan.

At first, the burnout victim will need to meet at least once a week with his "supervisor" to discuss the short-term plans and activities being pursued, and to evaluate progress and results. At some point, these meetings can be reduced to once or twice a month. They will, however, need to be continued for at least six months to one year.

It should be made clear that as the person with burnout begins to recover, he may actually reexperience the problems that first caused his burnout. Therefore, it is important to work with him to help him avoid repeating the same mistakes. As he recovers, he may be on the road to becoming a high achiever again, and high achievers tend to overextend themselves—which can start the process of burnout once more.

How to Avoid Burnout

We have looked at the causes of burnout and considered ways to overcome it. It is even more important, however, to know how to *prevent* this illness from infecting our lives. To avoid burnout, we must experience continuous spiritual, physical, emotional, and mental renewal.

(1) *Continuous spiritual renewal is the first and most important step in avoiding burnout.* We must always be developing and achieving spiritual goals designed to improve and strengthen our relationships with God. As Paul told the Ephesians: "Now your attitudes and thoughts must all be constantly changing for the better. Yes, you must be a new and different person, holy and good. Clothe yourself with this new nature" (4:23-24, TLB).

Spiritual stagnation leads to emotional deterioration. I can speak from personal experience: When you neglect your relationship with God, all other relationships suffer.

The time you spend with God is the most important time there is. So don't let anything or anyone interrupt that time. It is your greatest weapon against emotional burnout.

Remember, you can't keep giving of yourself without refilling your supply of spiritual strength. And as the psalmist tells us: "God is our refuge and strength, an ever present help in trouble" (Ps. 46:1).

(2) *Learn to pace yourself physically.* The high achiever frequently has problems learning to pace himself. However, to avoid burnout, you need to balance your work with play and rest. The author of Ecclesiastes points out that while there is a time to work, there also is a time to relax (3:1-8). People who avoid burnout have learned to apply this principle.

(3) *Guard your attitude: Focus on the positive happenings of the day.* In his Epistle to the Philippians, Paul advises believers to: "Fix your thoughts on what is true and good and right. Think about things that are pure and lovely, and dwell on the fine, good things in others. Think about all you can praise God for and be glad about" (4:8, TLB).

People who become burned-out emotionally have let themselves concentrate more on negative situations than on the positive. Yet focusing on the positive events of each day insures that the foundation of burnout—negative thoughts and attitudes—never is built.

(4) *Make sure you take a vacation every year.* For high achievers, a yearly vacation is an absolute must. It is far more than a reward for hard work. A vacation is one of the investments you make in yourself to guarantee that you'll be able to perform in the future. And it shouldn't be taken as a day here and there; it should cover an extended period of time—at least one week.

Leave your paperwork at home. Believe me, there is no such thing as a "working vacation." Unfortunately, when many business people I know get ready to squeeze in a day of "vacation," they load up their briefcases with enough work to keep them busy for two!

Most business people know how to work; but very few have learned how to play. It's a lesson worth learning.

(5) *Break out of routines.* The person who successfully avoids burnout is the individual who has learned how to avoid too many daily routines in his life. Find new and

different ways of doing old jobs. Adopt the motto, "There is always a better way of doing a job, and I'm going to find it."

A friend once told me, "When you're green, you're growing. But when you're ripe, you rot!" As long as you are growing and exploring new and better ways of meeting your daily schedules, you won't have to worry about burnout.

(6) *Constantly work on upgrading your goals.* The goals you set five years ago won't protect you from burnout today. Review your goals regularly. Change them. Expand them. Try new things. Develop new interests. In short, expand your horizons. Develop a broader base of interests. Don't just extend last year's goals.

(7) *Keep your life in balance.* Don't let your business run you—you should run your business! Keep a sense of balance between work, home, and play. In doing so, you will become a truly successful business person; you'll learn that you don't have to burn up all of your spiritual, emotional, and physical energies getting to the top.

Chapter Summary

Burnout is a type of job-related stress which is often caused by constant interaction with people and their problems. It is most prevalent among "high achievers" and those with intensively "people contact" jobs.

Burnout occurs when: (1) We try to manage our businesses all by ourselves; (2) Our accomplishments don't meet our expectations; (3) We lose a proper perspective of situations; (4) As Christians, we work harder and harder because we don't want to "let God down"; and (5) We conclude that it is impossible to accomplish certain tasks, and so we begin to hate what we are doing.

The following symptoms help us identify burnout: People experiencing burnout are very irritable. They become emotionally exhausted, which leads to physical exhaustion. They can no longer see things objectively; decisions are made strictly on feelings alone. People with burnout also lose all sense of courage, identity, and self-worth. They no longer are willing to take risks. Eventually, they may give up on life itself. If the person experiencing burnout is a Christian, he tends to get angry at God and to blame Him for his problems.

Observe the following steps when helping employees or co-workers with burnout: (1) People with burnout must have time away from the job; (2) This time away must not be for "self-evaluation," but for rest and relaxation; (3) They must start a physical exercise program; (4) When they return to work, their jobs must include new responsibilities; (5) They must experience immediate success; (6) They must develop a new purpose in life; (7) Finally, the person with burnout must become accountable to someone who will monitor his or her condition.

The irony of burnout is that people don't have to go through it—even if they *are* high achievers. To avoid this painful condition, we need to maintain a focus on spiritual renewal, and on improving our relationships with God.

We also must learn to pace ourselves physically; accordingly, we should be sure to take a vacation every year. We need time away from work for rest and relaxation. And it is very important that we avoid falling into the rut of monotonous daily routines.

Finally, we must protect our attitudes by focusing on the positive happenings of the day instead of the negative; we must constantly work to upgrade our goals; and we must keep our lives in balance.

Personal Application

1. Review the section entitled "What causes burnout?" If you or any of your employees are violating these principles, start looking for the symptoms of burnout listed on pages 153-155.

2. If you have employees who are experiencing burnout, begin implementing the recovery plan listed on pages 155-158.

3. You and every employee in your organization should follow the procedures for avoiding burnout as explained on pages 158-161.

11
Keeping Your Priorities Straight

George Preston fit the image of the modern, successful businessman. He was a member of the local country club and owned cabins in Colorado and Hawaii. Two Cadillacs and a four-wheel-drive pickup truck sat in his driveway. He kept his airplane at a small private airstrip—of which he was a part-owner. The word around town was, "If you need something done, see George Preston." He was very influential in local and state politics.

I first met George at a businessmen's luncheon. We became friends, and later I had an opportunity to conduct a small management development seminar for the supervisors in his company.

One day, George's secretary called me. She said that George was on his way back to town from the West Coast; he wanted to meet me for dinner at a restaurant he owned in Denver.

I got together with George later that evening. After we exchanged initial pleasantries, he became oddly quiet. "I suppose you're wondering why I asked you to meet me here," he finally mumbled. He paused, and I thought I detected a tear in the corner of his eye.

"Myron," he said, pushing his plate of half-eaten steak away from him, "my dad was a coal miner and we were poor. And when I say poor, I mean poor! So I decided as a kid that someday I was going to get away from that mining town, go to Denver, and make lots of money. And I did!

"I've spent the last thirty years busting my tail in this man's town," he continued. "And I've done alright. I probably could buy that whole little town in western Colorado where I was raised."

He paused, and big tears started rolling down both cheeks. George Preston was the last person I had ever expected to see cry. He was a friendly man, but gave the appearance of being tough and hard.

He looked up from the table and said, "I just came back from California, where I've been trying to talk my wife and sixteen-year-old daughter into coming back home."

After being out of town for a week on business, George had returned four days ago to find a note from his wife, Shirley; she said she couldn't take it anymore and was leaving him.

"I've always bought Shirley anything she wanted," he said. "I thought we were getting along fine. But today in California she told me I think more of my employees than I do of her because they make me money—and all she does is spend it.

"My family is the most important thing in my life," he added. "I did all this for them, but I guess I didn't do a very good job of letting them know."

George Preston's circumstances have been repeated countless times in the marketplaces of this country. In my years as a management consultant and businessman, I have met many people who awoke one day to find that the things they'd been giving their time, energy, and efforts to weren't really the most important ones. I would have to include myself on that list. Most of us find ourselves at one time or another drifting away from the things that are really important.

The Problem with Business People: Lack of a Balanced Life
Business people, more than any other group in our society, tend to lack *balance* in their lives. As we saw in the last chapter, keeping our lives in balance is one of the keys to avoiding burnout. It is also the key to real success in life.

George Preston was considered highly successful as a businessman. He was a failure, however, at home. Many business people like George know how to manage millions of dollars and hundreds of people at work, but don't know the first thing about "taking care of business" at home.

To be truly successful in life, we must be successful in *all* areas—not just making money. It is possible to make a million dollars and still fail at living.

Unfortunately for many business people, they have let their businesses run them instead of learning to run their businesses.

Martha Harris, for example, owns and operates one of the nicest gourmet restaurants in Arizona. She started in the restaurant business twenty years ago as a waitress and is a classic example of the self-made business person.

She told me, "I always wanted to own my own business because I wanted to be in control of my time. I wanted to be able to take time off without having to get someone else's approval. I wanted to make my own decisions and be my own boss."

She laughed and continued. "Now I own one of the best restaurants in town. I have the money to travel anywhere I want to go, but I am so tied down with this business I can't get away. I haven't had a vacation in three years, and it doesn't look like I'll be able to take one this year. I think I work for the business instead of it working for me."

Martha Harris' life is out of balance. She is devoting all her time and effort to the business and making money, and in the process she doesn't have any time left for herself.

Notice what Psalm 127:2 (TLB) says about spending all our time working in our businesses. "It is senseless for you to work so hard from early morning until late at night, fearing you will starve to death; for God wants His loved ones to get their proper rest."

God doesn't want us to spend excessive time running our businesses. He intends our lives to be balanced between work and rest. Most business people don't want to admit their lives are out of balance; but when a person spends ten to twelve hours a day, six days a week in his business, his life is unbalanced in favor of business.

What Is Really Important in Life?

George Preston discovered that his wife and daughter were more important than all the businesses, homes, cars, airplanes, and power his money could buy. But he found out too late.

As Christian business people operating in a marketplace where money and the things it can buy reign supreme, we must constantly guard our priorities. If we aren't careful, we too can wake up someday to discover that while we were grasping at the wrong priorities, the truly important things in life were slipping through our fingers.

What *is* really important in life? Many would say happiness; others, good health; some, financial security. All these are important, but according to the Bible, they are not the *most* important things in life.

The Bible teaches us that knowing and obeying God's Word are the most important things in life. Psalm 19:7-11 tells us that God's Word is perfect. It will protect us, make us wise, and give us joy. In fact, the passage says God's Word is more valuable than gold, warns us away from harm, and gives us success if we obey it.

Therefore, our number one priority in life should be to know and obey God's Word. It teaches us the key to having money and joy at the same time.

George Preston and Martha Harris learned how to make money, but wound up miserable. Money cost George his family and Martha her free time. As the Book of Job notes, "A man without God is trusting in a spider's web. Everything he counts on will collapse. If he counts on his home for security it won't last" (8:14-15, TLB).

Trusting in God and His Word is the most important thing in life. Yet most of us spend more time watching the news on TV each day than we do getting to know God and His Word!

God's words to the church in Laodicea could just as easily have been written to the Christian business people of today: "You say, 'I am rich; I have acquired wealth and do not need a thing.' But you do not realize that you are wretched, pitiful, poor, blind, and naked" (Rev. 3:17).

How Do We Know What Our Priorities Are?

We all recognize the need for priorities in our lives. A few of us have actually gone through the exercise of identifying and writing them down.

There are two kinds of priorities: real and imagined. Sometimes it is difficult to tell the difference. Both can be identified and written on a piece of paper. Both can be discussed. We can even think we are accomplishing both.

But the things we spend our time doing reflect our *real* priorities. Real priorities may or may not be written or even clearly identified in our minds. But we know they are the real ones because we are spending our time doing them.

Things we talk about doing, plan to do, want to do...but don't do are *imagined* priorities. They are not real ones.

We may not want to admit it, but we always find time to do the things that are important to us. We can talk all we want to about how important our families are or how important God and His work are to us. But if our families and God always tend to get our "leftover" time, they are only *imagined* priorities—not real ones. To repeat: Our real priorities are things we spend time doing; imagined priorities are things we *say* are important, but don't *do*.

Notice Jesus' words recorded in Matthew about the Pharisees: "These people honor Me with their lips, but their hearts are far from Me" (15:8). The Pharisees imagined or thought God was their top priority, but their actions proved He wasn't. They gave lip service to God, but didn't give Him their hearts.

We make time commitments to our real priorities, but our imagined priorities get only lip service. The tragedy of imagined priorities is that they deceive us. We think we are doing things we aren't, that we're committed to things we're not.

For example, George Preston's family was an imagined priority. He gave lip service to their being the most important thing in his life. He even believed it was true himself. But he didn't give his family his time.

You only give time to your real priorities. You may give money and verbal support to imagined priorities; but time, your most prized possession, is reserved only for the things that truly matter to you.

If you want to know what your real priorities are, look at where you spend your time—not what you say or how you spend your money!

The Things That Compete for Priority in Your Life

We may know God's Word should be our top priority as Christians, but there are many things in the marketplace trying to crowd God out of the picture. For example, Mark tells us, "But all too quickly the attractions of this world and the delights of wealth, and the search for success and lure of nice things come in and crowd out God's message" (4:19, TLB).

What a description of modern Western society! This verse provides graphic examples of the things that tend to keep God's Word from being a priority in our lives. Notice that each distraction constantly confronts business people in the marketplace:

- The attractions of this world.
- Delight in wealth.
- Search for success.
- The lure of nice things.

Let's examine each of these more closely.

The attractions of this world. The world is attracted to things like power, fame, prestige, and control. People in the marketplace generally put more emphasis on these things than on God and His Word.

Rehoboam, King Solomon's son, is a biblical example of such a person. After Solomon's death, Rehoboam became king. As 2 Chronicles 12:1 (TLB) says, "But just when Rehoboam was at the height of his popularity and power he abandoned the Lord, and the people followed him in this sin."

Delight in wealth. Most people in the marketplace put far greater priority on acquiring wealth than on knowing and obeying God and His Word. Acquiring wealth takes so much of some people's time and energy, in fact, that they don't have *any* resources left for God. They may go to church for an hour on Sunday and place a dollar in the offering plate; they may even stand up in church and say how they love God and are committed to Him. But the remaining 167 hours a week are devoted to figuring out how to make more money.

These people have an imagined priority of putting God first in their lives, but their real priority is acquiring wealth. That is where they spend all their time.

Deuteronomy warns, "For when you have become full and prosperous and have built fine homes to live in, and when your flocks and herds have become very large, and your silver and gold have multiplied, that is the time to watch out that you don't become proud, and forget the Lord your God" (8:12-14, TLB).

Search for success. Of all the people in the Bible, wouldn't Solomon be able to handle success and remain true to God? After all, God declared that Solomon was the wisest man who ever lived. Yet, 1 Kings 10-11 shows Solomon building a successful kingdom—only to begin drifting away from God.

There is nothing wrong with success. God promises certain

kinds of success if we continually put Him first and obey His Word. Joshua indicates, "Do not let this Book of the Law depart from your mouth; meditate on it day and night, so that you may be careful to do everything written in it. Then you will be prosperous and successful" (1:8).

In other words, this verse says that being committed to knowing and obeying God's Word is the way to be successful *and* faithful to God at the same time.

The lure of nice things. Like wealth and success, the lure of luxury and the acquisition of nice things can throw us out of balance. We wind up spending so much time trying to "keep up with the Joneses" that we forget our commitment to God.

The tragedy is that "things" alone never give us real joy and peace. God promises that if you "Seek first His kingdom and His righteousness... all these things will be given to you as well" (Matt. 6:33).

When we know and obey God and His Word, He meets all our emotional as well as physical needs. As Psalm 29:11 says, "The Lord gives strength to His people; the Lord blesses His people with peace." Psalm 119:165 tells us the source of that peace: "Great peace have they who love Your Law, and nothing can make them stumble."

Getting Your Life in Balance

It isn't always easy for business people to keep their lives in balance. But it is absolutely essential if we want to have the abundant life Jesus promised us in John 10:10.

To keep our lives in balance, we must remove the garbage and insignificant rubble from our daily routines. We must identify the things that are really important and focus on them. In other words, we must *make time* for the right priorities.

George Preston lost his family because he failed to make time in his schedule for them. Everything else took precedence over them when it came to dividing up George's day.

One "law" of time management states that *80 percent of our success comes from 20 percent of our activity.* That also means that 80 percent of our activity only produces 20 percent of our success. Unproductive activity is robbing us of time that should be spent on important priorities.

The beautiful flowers in our "gardens of life" will wither and die if we allow the weeds and thistles to grow too thick. Only we can pull them out.

Keeping our lives in balance requires regularly pulling out the weeds and thistles so that the flowers have a chance to grow and bloom. Insignificant activities that take up time but contribute almost nothing to our success must be weeded out and thrown away. We must focus on the significant, letting the insignificant die from lack of attention.

We must also learn to say no to some worthwhile causes. As mentioned earlier, most business people are high achievers. They have a knack for getting things done quickly. As a result, they are constantly bombarded by people who represent all kinds of good causes wanting "just a little" of their time.

For example, the XYZ Fund may be a good cause and need help in promotion. But is being chairman of the local fund drive this year as important as spending some quality time with your spouse and kids?

I don't believe it is. That doesn't mean the XYZ Fund isn't a good cause. But you can't get involved in every good activity that comes along. If you do, you will never have time to get involved in the *best* ones. Why settle for good activities when you can have the best?

To have time for the best things in life, we must practice "selective involvement"—and learn to say no to most of the merely good things. It's a matter of priorities.

Many business people miss the really great times in life because they develop the Settle-for Syndrome. They settle for a day off now and then, rather than taking a week or two with the family for a *real* vacation. They settle for a quick lunch with the spouse at a hamburger stand between business appointments instead of clearing the calendar for an entire evening and going out to dinner as a couple at a nice restaurant.

If we want to keep our priorities straight and our lives in balance, we can't allow ourselves to catch the Settle-for Syndrome. It's an epidemic in the marketplace. Most business people have it, and if you hang around them too much you are likely to catch it. The only way to avoid Settle-for Syndrome is to know exactly what your real priorities are, write them down, review them regularly, and plan specifically how you will accomplish them.

The alternative is to lose your right to choose. In other words, *if you don't know what is most important in your life, you will always wind up doing the things most important to other people.* Geraldene Hopkins, wife of a business friend, told me during a Christmas party, "Lloyd [her husband] lets everyone lead him around by the nose. People are always coming around, saying they just have to have his help on this important project or that important project." She handed me another glass of red punch and continued. "I guess he must feel their projects are more important than his. The problem is, he's always so busy helping other people he never has time to help *us!* Sometimes I feel like he thinks other people and their problems are more important than I am."

I'd seen Lloyd in action, and his wife was right. It didn't matter that Lloyd had told me several times over lunch what a great wife he had. If she really had been a top priority in his life, he would have helped her with her important projects also.

It isn't what you say that counts: It's what you *do* that proves where your priorities are—or whether you have any. And if you don't develop your own priorities, someone else will develop them for you. In most cases they will be for that someone's benefit—not yours.

If you want to know a person's values, look at his priorities. If you want to know his priorities, look at how he spends his time. Your own actions are a statement to others concerning the most important things in your life.

Priorities are the "guard rails" on the road of life; they keep us on track. They also keep us from getting bogged down in the mire of ineffectiveness. How far and how fast you travel in life will depend on how faithful you are at developing and maintaining your priorities.

Chapter Summary

Most business people have problems keeping their lives in balance. Their businesses frequently become all-important, crowding out other priorities such as family, friends, hobbies, and leisure time.

Our priorities tell us and others what is really important to us. As Job 8:14 indicates, God should be our most important priority; we can't count on anything else for security.

There are two kinds of priorities: *real* and *imagined.* Real priorities are the things we spend our time doing. Real priorities do not necessarily have to be written down or clearly identified; we know they are real because we give them our most prized possession—our time.

On the other hand, things we talk about doing, plan to do, want to do, but *don't* do are imagined priorities. Imagined priorities may be written down and discussed regularly, but if we never *do* them they aren't actually priorites.

According to Jesus, God sometimes loses first place in our lives when "the attractions of this world and the delights of wealth, and the search for success and lure of nice things come in and crowd out God's message" (Mark 4:19, TLB).

It isn't always easy for business people to keep balanced; but. we must to experience the "abundant life."

Some say 80 percent of our success comes from only 20 percent of our activity. To keep balanced, we must focus on removing the unproductive activity from our days—to make more time for the really important things.

We must also learn to say no to worthwhile causes that hinder us from accomplishing our own priorities. Just because an activity is worthwhile doesn't mean we should do it. Sometimes we wind up settling for second best, when with a little more effort we could have had the best.

The purpose of priorities is to help us live the best lives possible. Without priorities, we aren't really living at all.

Personal Application
1. Evaluate your priorities. Are they real or imagined?

2. Write out your priorities. Those involving the family should be done jointly. Develop a plan of action for pursuing these goals.
3. Pick a date to review this chapter as a way to help keep you on track with your priorities.

12
Reaching Your Full Potential in the Marketplace

On May 25, 1961 President John F. Kennedy set forth one of the greatest challenges ever made to a nation. Before a joint session of the United States Congress, he declared, "I believe this nation should commit itself to achieving the goal, before this decade is out, of landing a man on the moon and returning him safely to earth."

Sending a man to the moon and back seemed impossible to most people. It was something to read about in Buck Rogers science fiction stories, but we "knew better" than to believe it could actually happen.

As we know now, it not only happened—it happened just 8 years and 56 days after Kennedy issued his challenge. On July 20, 1969 at 10:56 P.M. Eastern Daylight Time, Neil Armstrong became the first human to set foot on the moon. And of course he and his fellow astronauts returned safely to earth.

Man's Potential for Achievement

Man's trip to the moon and back demonstrated several things: (1) Space travel to other heavenly bodies is possible, (2) Unbelievable things can be accomplished when an entire nation rallies behind a goal, and (3) The potential for human achievement is almost without limits.

During the past two decades, the world has experienced a technological explosion. Every day brings phenomenal new discoveries and inventions.

I recently read, for example, about a new type of aircraft under investigation and preliminary development by Lockheed-California Company. Half conventional jetliner and half spaceship, the craft is called The Trans-Atmospheric Vehicle. It could fly at "low" altitudes like our conventional jetliners or climb seventy miles to the very edge of outer space.

The "plane" could travel from Los Angeles to New York in *twelve minutes;* from Los Angeles to Australia in *thirty minutes*; and around the world in just *ninety minutes!* If ready for operation in the 1990s as expected, the craft will revolutionize air travel—and reduce the length of a world-circling trip to that of a Sunday afternoon drive.

Both the Old Testament (Genesis 11:6) and the New Testament (Matthew 17:20) point out that man can accomplish anything God allows. Christ confirmed the role faith can play in that process when He said, "I tell you the truth, if you have faith as small as a mustard seed, you can say to this mountain, 'Move from here to there' and it will move. Nothing will be impossible for you" (Matt. 17:20).

I've never studied Hebrew or Greek, but it seems to me that when God says, "Nothing will be impossible," He means *nothing!* God has created unlimited potential in us.

The Role Your Attitude Plays in Developing Your Potential
Chapter eight described the importance of our attitudes in dealing with failure. Our attitudes are equally important when it comes to developing our full potentials.

Your attitude toward God, yourself, and your potential is a key to determining what you accomplish in life. Notice the wisdom of Proverbs: "As in water face answers to face, so the mind of man reflects the man" (27:19, RSV).

History has given us countless examples of people who overcame great obstacles, moving on to achieve big things because their attitudes were right. An Egyptian peasant boy, for example, became an officer in the Egyptian army—only to be falsely accused of treason and thrown into prison. After spending several years in a cell, he went on to become Egypt's president. He was Anwar Sadat.

Sadat could have given up on life because of his prison record, but he didn't. He believed he could make a contribution to his country, and his attitude carried him to the top.

Albert Einstein failed his college entrance exams. But he didn't let that stop him. He went on to develop the theory of relativity, and was recognized as one of the greatest minds in history.

If we think we can't succeed, we won't; if we think we can, we will find a way. At some point along our achievement curve most of us conclude, "I could never see myself accomplishing *that!*" So we stop trying. It is far better to aim high and hit a little low than not to aim and miss altogether.

For example, as I was completing my graduate work at Central Missouri State University, a friend told me Eastern Montana College was looking for someone to manage a large federally funded educational program. As I read the job description and requirements, I discovered they wanted someone with a Ph.D.

My friend and I had only masters degrees, but we wanted higher education jobs in Montana. When I asked him if he planned to apply for the job, he said, "Oh, no! They want someone with a doctor's degree. They would never hire me."

I told him I was going to send them a resumé; at the worst, they might say I wasn't qualified. My friend snickered at me and said I was just wasting a stamp. "They probably won't even answer your letter," he said with a taunting laugh.

I mailed the resumé anyway. A few days later I received a call from the college telling me I wasn't qualified for the job I had applied for. But would I be interested in managing a smaller federal program in their education department that only required a masters degree?

Two weeks later I was living in Montana, working at that new job.

When I told my friend about my new position and salary, he hung his head. He had just signed a contract to teach junior high science for half the salary. He'd earned better grades than I had in graduate school and had previous experience working in federal projects; had he applied; he probably would have been hired. But his attitude had kept him from even trying to get the job.

Let me say it again: It is far better to aim high and hit a little low than not to aim and miss altogether! And the height of our aim is determined by our attitudes.

The Importance of Listening to God

We have already seen examples of people who accomplished great things on their own. But without God a person never reaches his or her *full* potential. He may build a large and profitable business. He may become the leader in his field. But he will never become all he can be apart from a close relationship with God.

Paul recognized this. That is why he said, "I can do everything through Him who gives me strength" (Phil. 4:13). Paul knew there was nothing he couldn't do with God's help.

Christ Himself confirmed Paul's claim: "Everything is possible for him who believes" (Mark 9:23).

Developing a personal relationship with God makes His power available to us. That means talking to Him every day— and listening when He is talking to us. Unfortunately, most of us get so busy with our day-to-day activities that we don't listen to God when He tries to help us become productive. As my friend Russ Johnston says, "Most of us have our heads so full of our own ideas and activities we would need a hearing aid to hear God."

If we expect to develop our full potential we must learn to listen to God. "Call to Me and I will answer you and tell you great and unsearchable things you do not know" (Jer. 33:3). God not only wants to talk to us; He wants to reveal great things.

Businessman Jack Thompson learned that through experience. As owner of a feed lot and meat packing business in western Nebraska, Jack was approached by a group of businessmen who wanted him to build a large feed lot several times the size of the one he'd been operating for years. Sales projections showed that the rising price of beef would allow him to pay for the expansion in a very short time. And the other men had already arranged for a buyer for the beef.

"The deal really looked good," Jack said later. "They were

willing to invest in the project, and it appeared we could all make a lot of money. I told them I would have to pray about it before I could give them my final answer. But I explained that the deal sure looked good."

Jack went home and prayed for direction. "I woke up in the middle of the night with the strongest feeling I should turn the deal down," he recalled. "I couldn't understand why God would not want me to do the project, because it looked like such a good deal. The projections indicated I would make more money in a couple of years' time than I had made in the last ten!"

Jack shook his head, remembering. "The hardest thing I ever did was to tell those guys no. But I thank God I listened to Him—because within a year the bottom dropped out of the cattle market and I would have lost everything I had."

Jack discovered an important principle through that experience. "I've learned it sure pays to listen to God, even when the numbers look like it's a good deal! God knows the future and I don't. And as long as I listen to Him it always turns out for my best."

Our potential for achievement is in direct proportion to our ability to make right decisions. That is why the Christian has greater potential for achievement than the non-Christian; if the Christian will only listen to God, he can make the right decision. God not only knows what is best in the current situation; He knows what is best in light of the future.

The best market projections in the world can't come close to God's accuracy in predicting the future. That's why it's so important to listen to God—not just to Wall Street.

We should not only listen to God, but also take action when He tells us to do so. His timing is perfect.

Art Fowler is a friend who knows that truth. A professional consultant who lives in Colorado, he told me over a cup of coffee, "You know, I've sure been learning that it pays to always listen to what God tells you to do."

Then he told me how a few weeks before he had been invited to Mesa, Arizona to conduct a seminar. Before the seminar, however, he needed to take a trip to Denver. As he prepared to go to the mile-high city, he suddenly felt God wanted him to take the bus instead of driving his car.

Thinking that was rather strange, Art tried to dismiss it from his mind—but couldn't. "I can't explain it," he said later, "but I just felt compelled to take the bus instead of driving my car." Wondering why God would want him to take the bus, he nevertheless decided to go ahead and do it.

On the way to Denver, Art sat right behind the bus driver and struck up a conversation with him. When Art told the driver about the seminar in Mesa, Arizona the next week, the driver said he had been to that town many times. His brother lived in Mesa, he explained.

Art got the brother's name. Later, in Mesa, he called the man, introduced himself, and made an appointment to meet him.

"The guy was reluctant to meet with me," Art told me. "In fact, I had to call him three times before he would agree to meet for coffee."

When they got together, Art explained again that he was a consultant and counselor who helped professionals learn how to handle stress. The man told Art he was a businessman and pilot—and was undergoing a great deal of stress in his business and at home.

"I began to talk to him about God and explain that He was

the answer to his problems," Art said. As he did so, the man began to cry.

"If you had called me any other day except today, I would not have listened to you," the man said. "But I have so many problems I have to do something to solve them."

Before they left that coffee shop, the man bowed his head and accepted Jesus Christ as Saviour. After praying, the man said, "My wife has been praying for me for years. And she didn't want me to come to meet you today. Boy! I can't wait to tell her God sent you here to answer her prayers."

If Art Fowler had not listened to God's urging to take the bus to Denver instead of driving his car, Art would not have met the bus driver or his brother in Mesa. While Art was deciding to listen to God and ride the bus, God was urging the man's wife to pray for her husband. And while she was praying for her husband, God was creating situations in his business that made him ready to listen to the Gospel when Art arrived.

Isn't it amazing how God will tell a man in Colorado to take a bus ride to Denver so that he can answer the prayers of a wife in Arizona?

As Art told his story, I sat there and wondered how many opportunities I had missed. How many people had I let down just because I was too busy to listen to God? Jack Thompson and Art Fowler are living proof that we accomplish far more by listening to God than just to ourselves and others.

Art is a classic example of how God can use a business to accomplish His work—if we will only listen to our senior business partner. God provided the business for Art so that he could accomplish the spiritual business for God. You can't find a better example of teamwork anywhere.

Ask God to Expand Your Vision

How big are your dreams? What do you really want to accomplish in life? To develop your full potential, you must begin seeing your potential the way God sees it. We looked at Ephesians 3:20 (TLB) in an earlier chapter, but it deserves our attention again:

Now glory be to God who by His mighty power at work within us is able to do far more than we would ever dare to ask or even dream of—infinitely beyond our highest prayers, desires, thoughts, or hopes.

In this verse God is challenging us to expand our vision and faith and believe Him for bigger things.

A friend of mine, Marv Heidelburg, buys and sells real estate. He told me, "I used to pray and ask God to help me find an old 'junker' of a house that I could buy for a few thousand dollars, fix up, and sell for a decent profit. I made a fairly decent living doing that for years."

He grinned as he continued. "Then one day I read Ephesians 3:20 and realized it didn't matter to God whether I prayed for a junker house or a junker apartment complex; He had the power to do both."

Today Marv buys large commercial complexes and shopping centers that have been run down. He fixes them up, gets new tenants in the store spaces, and then sells the complexes. "It's all a matter of zeros," he told me. "There is no limit to the number of zeros God can handle. It all depends on how many *I* have the faith to handle."

Do you want to develop your full potential in and out of the marketplace? Then begin meditating on Ephesians 3:20, and ask God to expand your vision of what is possible. You are limited only by the size of your vision and what you are willing to believe God will do through you.

Get on Your Heart the Things That Are on God's Heart

If you want to develop your full potential you must be willing to "team up" with God. He must have more than the title of "senior partner" in your business. He must actually have "controlling interest" in you *and* your business.

Because God's top priority is people, you must develop a heart for people too. When you put God first in your life and business, you are putting others' interests before your own.

It is impossible to serve God and not serve people.

> For I was hungry and you gave Me something to eat, I was thirsty and you gave Me something to drink, I was a stranger and you invited Me in .... Then the righteous will answer Him, "Lord, when did we see You hungry and feed You, or thirsty and give You something to drink? When did we see You a stranger and invite You in...?" The King will reply, "I tell you the truth, whatever you did for one of the least of these brothers of Mine, you did for Me" (Matt. 25:35-40).

Going to the moon isn't nearly as great an achievement as listening to God and bringing the Good News about Jesus Christ to a man in Mesa, Arizona. Designing an aircraft capable of traveling from Los Angeles to New York in twelve minutes doesn't please God nearly as much as a feed lot owner's request for and obedience to His direction.

As Christian business people, you and I have unlimited potential. But it will only be fulfilled as we listen to God and His Word—instead of the voices in the marketplace.

Chapter Summary

Jesus said, "Everything is possible for him who believes" (Mark 9:23). The Bible makes it clear that people have unlimited creative potential. Modern technological advances tend to verify that idea.

Still, the Christian has greater potential for achievement than the non-Christian because God is available to direct and protect him. God wants to guide our plans and decisions, but only if we are willing to listen to Him and obey His instructions.

We must also have a positive attitude about ourselves and what we are capable of achieving. It is far better to aim high and hit a little low, than not to aim and miss altogether.

If we expect to achieve our full potential, we must ask God to expand our visons of what can be accomplished. Paul tells us, "Now glory be to God who by His mighty power at work within us is able to do far more than we would ever dare to ask or even dream of—infinitely beyond our highest prayers, desires, thoughts, or hopes" (Eph. 3:20, TLB).

This verse makes it very clear that God wants us to expand our faith and thinking. He wants us to realize just how much power He makes available to us to achieve our full potential in and out of the marketplace.

Personal Application

1. What is your attitude toward yourself, God, and your potential for achievement? Read Genesis 11:6, Matthew 17:20, and Mark 9:23. What impact do these verses have on your vision of potential achievements?

2. How much time do you spend each day talking to God about your plans and decisions? How much do you spend

listening to God's answers? Do you need to spend more time listening?

3. Read and meditate on Ephesians 3:20. Review your current goals for your business and ask God whether they should be expanded in light of this verse. Do whatever He tells you.

13
Conclusion

For the past few years I have been saying, *"If you want to know what the standards of the Christian community will be in ten years—look out on the street corners of the marketplace today!"* Unfortunately, that statement is becoming more of a reality every day. It is getting harder and harder to distinguish between the business philosophies and practices of Christians and non-Christians.

This book has not been easy to write. I have tried to challenge you and myself to awaken from our complacency —even apathy—and deal with some of the Bible's toughest passages and principles as they relate to the Christian business person in today's marketplace. God has shown me many areas in my own life in which I am falling far short of what He expects from me as a Christian business person.

At the beginning of the book I guessed that for some of you I might raise more questions than I answered. I hope that hasn't been the case. I am aware, however, that many of the points will need to be considered with much prayer. I truly hope you will seek God's mind and will for you and your business concerning each of the issues discussed in this book, and not just take the word of this management consultant from Colorado Springs.

For thirteen years I have been crisscrossing this country, doing management consulting and conducting management seminars for all kinds of businesses and organizations. It has been encouraging to meet so many Christians in the marketplace. But it has been equally discouraging—at times depressing—to see so few Christian business people actively applying biblical principles of business in their corners of the marketplace.

During the last few years, however, there seems to be a spiritual awakening occurring among Christian business people. There is a growing interest and hunger to know and apply God's principles of business to their day-to-day situations.

All over the country individuals and small groups of Christian business people are beginning to come out of their warehouses, production areas, and offices, banding together to learn how to more effectively light the lost and frustrated marketplace. Many of these small groups are blossoming into organizations with dedicated leadership.

One of the most effective organizations for Christian business owners and chief executive officers that I have ever encountered is the Fellowship of Companies for Christ (FCC). Many of the ideas for this book came from the contact I've had with FCC and those involved in it. If you are a business owner or CEO I strongly encourage you to contact this organization for more information:

Fellowship of Companies for Christ
61 Perimeter Park, N.E.
Atlanta, GA 30341
Telephone: (404) 457-9700

The Fellowship of Companies for Christ is an organization designed just for business owners and CEOs. Its purpose is to help businesses apply biblical principles of business on a day-to-day basis in the marketplace. The organization conducts conferences and has audio and video cassette tapes available.

If you know of other organizations designed to help equip the Christian business person to operate his or her business according to biblical principles, I would be most interested in hearing about them. People constantly ask me about organizations of this nature in their areas, and I would be delighted to pass information on to those who might benefit from such groups—formal or informal.

I sincerely pray that God will use you and your business to make a lasting impact for Him in the marketplace.